A Periodic Table of Greek Mythology

Working Classicists

Edited by Miri Teixeira

Contubernales Books

2024

ISBN: 978-1-961822-16-0

Cover Illustration by Garrett Dome

Periodic Table Design by Cora Beth Fraser

Typeset in EB Garamond.

Contents

Contributors

In Order of Appearance

Joel Gordon, Gregory Rowe, Ellie Mackin Roberts, Riley Gombis, Brendon Little, Zara Naveed, Craig Melia, Matthew Speight, Jenna Glassburner, Lucy E. Farnan, LJ Trafford, Naomi Rebis, Ben Cassell, Oliver Maynard, Dr Kerry Phelan, Lucy Angel, Dr Christina Hotalen, Ciara Meehan, Mike Delayo, Chris McGonigle, Aidan Scully, Christina Osborn, Peter Wright, Alexandra Sills, Lorna Lee, Ashley Ann Cassidy, C. M. Kosemen, Tyler Kelly, Baily D. Peters, Ryan Marc Williamson, Connor Hickey, Sascha Engel, Cora Beth Fraser, Alice Main, Alisha Dodds, Megan Mahoney, Lauren Murphy, Liv Albert, George McAdam-Cross, Tobias Fulton, Amber Taylor, Alicia Matz, Carys Hughes, Tanika Koosmen, Yentl Love, Anna Fernández Iglesias, Mike Beer, Ross McGovern, Evie Chandler, Samuel Azzopardi, Suzanne Graham, Aneirin C. Pendragon, Katherine Livingston, Carlotta Vincenzi, Derek McCann, Jacqueline Munro, Robyn Hayward, Kate Minniti, Ellana Rose Thornton-Wheybrew, Daniel Galef, Zoe Lister, Natasha Hershaw, Simon Trafford, Georgina Homer, Amanda D. Binns, Talia R. BarNoy, Aimee Hinds Scott, Isabel Hood, Dr Jeremy Swist, Francesco Paolo Dal Rio, Amanda Rivera, Chrissie Downton, Doug Henning, Ciaran Tolland, Dr. Shelby Judge, Midah Guilbaud-Walter, Douglas Jones, Dr. Maciej Paprocki, Adam Thain, Trevor Culley, Marios Koutsoukos, Jessica McKenzie, Charlotte Gregory, Sierra P. Jones, Dries Cuykx, Emily Small, Alexia Burrows Charalambidou, Louise O'Brien, Dr. Alex Imrie, Aidan Mooney, Vicki Feltham, Allison Menai Newbould, Sol A. Cardenas, George Connor, Ross Clare, Keeli Cadwell, Lucy Neill, Regina Nagan, Alexander Vandewalle, Susan Deacy, Tom Bright, Caitlin Yool, Livia Adams, Justin L. Biggi, Aiden Cattanach, Ashleigh Hamilton, Colin Gough, Mehr-un-Nisa Syed, Rachel Stott, Kenna Gibson, Madelaine Sacco, Robert Caudill, Emily Bausher, Julie Levy, Ella Quinn, Echo Smith, Princess O'Nika Auguste.

Edited by Miri Teixeira. Fact-checked by Carlotta Vincenzi.

Acknowledgements

Jaqueline Munro *for volunteering with Working Classicists so enthusiastically and blessing us all with your wit, insight, and dedication.* **Albert A'Hara** *for giving your life to Classical Studies and Latin, embodying a passion and belief in equality that will inspire generations to come.* **Dr. Alex Imrie** *for being a mentor, a support, and a friend.* **Naomi Upward** and **Ross McGovern** *for believing in Working Classicists, and us, before we'd even started.*

A Word from the Editor

When we started Working Classicists in 2021, our initial aim was to have a simple webpage with some links to resources. The goal eventually grew loftier, to promote the study of Ancient History, Classical Studies, Latin, and Ancient Greek in state schools across the UK, and provide a community for Classicists and enthusiasts who don't come from a background of privilege. We never expected it to snowball into a network of tens of thousands of people, including members, supporters, and contributors from all across the world.

The website now hosts an array of free resources, recommendations for further study (or Classics-based fun), and avenues of support – including an online Zine which publishes exciting articles from up-and-coming authors and researchers of all disciplines. We've published theatre reviews, ancient recipes, video game run-downs, personal reflections, and more. We have a Discord server, where fellow Working Classicists can search for jobs, ask questions, and enter giveaways. We've started rolling out outreach programs that benefit pupils and teachers at state schools across Scotland. In short, we've got a lot going on.

But however much Working Classicists has changed and grown, our aim has remained the same. We believe that whatever background you are from, you should be able to pursue an enthusiasm in these subjects, as a hobby, course of study, or profession. We believe that significant redistribution of the knowledge wealth in this area hinges on developing networks of connection between individuals and organisations who have difficulty in accessing it.

University courses in these disciplines seem to overflow with alumni from independent schools, and this can be hugely alienating for those who went to the local comp. It is estimated that 7% of the UK population attend private schools, but the majority of students in the field of Classics come from the private sector. This is simply not egalitarian. This is not equality of choice or opportunity.

The label of Working Classicist is a way for a whole group of people – amateurs, academics and professionals – to identify themselves with pride, and to make connections with others from similar backgrounds. It is a way of overcoming the imposter syndrome which so many Classicists from the

93% feel.

This book is an opportunity for us to share what we have always known, that to be a skilled academic, a passionate Classicist, and an engaging professional writer, you do not need to have come from a private school or an upper-middle class background.

Within our boundaries of how we define class, which you can find on our website, this book is a glorious anomaly in the field. Just under 80% of the 117 writers in this book come from a working class background, and 81% attended a state school of some kind.

If you're the sort of person who enjoys statistics, here are some more: 48.7% of the writers in this book identify as female, while 29.1% identify as male, and 15.4% as non-binary. Through further self-identification we know that 58 writers are members of the LGBTQIA+ community, 58 writers are disabled, 43 writers are neurodiverse, and 12 writers self-identified as BAME or POC. In this book, the usual minority in Classics has become the majority, proving the enrichment on offer when diverse voices are uplifted.

Classicists from across the globe are represented in this book, with many writing in their second language. People from all backgrounds were invited to participate. As such, 46.2% of our writers are educated to a postgraduate level, while 24.8% have undergraduate degrees. 17.9% have doctorates, and 6% stated high school qualifications as their highest level of formal education.

When editing the book, I tried not to change the voice of the individual. As is inevitable in a project with this many people, there is a degree of repetition between some 'elements', but each writer put forward their own spin on characters, places, and concepts. Errors and snags were caught (I hope!), translations into English undertaken, and footnotes made, but each piece was crafted by the author credited at the end of every page. Each person's own perspective and narrative style should, therefore, shine through, their unique tones creating a chorus of voices. I am incredibly grateful to, and proud of, every single writer who contributed to this project.

This book is more than a beginners guide to ancient Greek mythology, but also acts as a vision of the creative talent and academic wit that the field of Classics would benefit from if it were more freely open and accessible to these communities. The voices are out there, you just have to listen.

Miri Teixeira

Introduction

By George Connor

I F YOU ARE NEW to Greek mythology, then you are incredibly lucky, in the same way that any person is lucky at the start of a long, interesting journey: there is so much for you to learn, to love, to be inspired by, and so many stories waiting to unfold for you. I hope that this book sparks the Promethean fire of curiosity in you, and you will enjoy a lifelong enthusiasm for these characters and their stories.

On the other hand, if you are a bit longer in the tooth when it comes to the thrills of Greek mythology, and have traversed this road before, there is still a lot to be excited by in these pages. Etymologies, explanations, correlations with history, and strange connections to the modern day... You have here a cornucopia of trivia which will delight you.

Finding out about the world of Greek myths was not something I had access to when I was at my (state) school, and this is no doubt an experience common to most of the people reading this book. Since the 1990s, state school Classics (the study of the ancient world and its languages) has been in decline in the United Kingdom, meaning that fewer and fewer school pupils were able to play in its marvellous sandpit of magic and drama.

It has also meant that fewer and fewer Classics teachers were trained, which meant fewer schools could offer Classical subjects. A cycle which diminished Classics until its near-extinction.

In June of 2021, Miri and I founded Working Classicists, a group dedicated to reviving Classics for people who attend, or attended, a state school. We felt strongly that the discipline needed a distinct voice, shouting about the difficulties and injustices (and benefits) of coming from a working class background.

Since then, we have published more than a hundred articles by writers of all backgrounds, spoken at the Classical Association conference at Cambridge, delivered outreach talks in public libraries, launched the Working Classicists Awards, and tried to provide a community for people with a love for the ancient world, but who have felt excluded from it.

Our project has been funded only by our own wages (I am a state school teacher, while Miri is a copywriter - we're not loaded), and the occasional generous donations of our supporters.

In mid-2023, we were surprised to be approached by a publisher and given carte blanche to write a book of our own choosing. It's not an email you get every day, but it's one you don't ignore.

We - like a lot of people - have a lot of ideas for books we would love to write, but we knew instinctively that this opportunity should be shared.

Within a very short time we settled on this Periodic Table of Greek Mythology, an opportunity not only to write about something we love, but to bring together 117 different Working Classicists and put some of our ethos down on paper.

As a teacher, I have used a version of the table in my classes for nearly ten years, using each "element" as a launchpad for discussion, research, games, and quizzes. Picking a selection of element cards off the wall was always a sign that the day's class was going to head in some unexpected directions.

Historically, the Periodic Table format has been used to categorise and organise, giving clarity and order to often diffuse information. The version you now hold is an attempt to make the sometimes overwhelming scale of the world of Greek mythology seem a little less daunting.

If you are reading the stories for the first time it can be hard to remember who everyone is, and how they connect to everyone else. If you don't know your Tantalus from your Ophion, then this book should help you to see who is who. You'll not find everyone here, but just a handful of the characters that make up the rich history of ancient Greek folklore and religion.

In the future, we have aspirations to produce more resources for schools, to write at least one textbook, to publish more and more marginalised writers, and to provide practical, emotional and financial help for people who struggle to gain full access to the Classics.

We hope there will be other books from Working Classicists, too, but if this is where our publishing career begins and ends, we are very proud of what these pages contain.

The writers represented here have produced a wonderful, varied and interesting collection of biographies: more than a hundred different voices, offering more than a hundred perspectives on more than a hundred characters from Greek mythology. This book literally would not be in your hands right now were it not for their generous contributions.

These pages are a totem to the love we all feel for Greek mythology, for its endless capacity to provide meaning, inspiration, solace, and rollicking good stories; it is a raised fist to say that Classics belongs to everyone, not just those lucky enough to attend certain schools or universities; it is a collective work, reflecting the values which Working Classicists wishes to see in the world: accessibility, collaboration, enthusiasm, erudition, and joy!

There are a lot of people to thank for their contributions to what you now hold. Contubernales, our publishers, for going far out on a limb and making an offer we absolutely could not refuse; Dr. Cora Beth Fraser for her gorgeous poster which accompanies this book; and the dozens and dozens and dozens of writers who stepped-up to make a contribution. I also want to thank the person responsible for corralling everything, and keeping the project going, Miri Teixeira, who worked for countless hours above her day job to put this book together.

George Connor

A Periodic Table of Greek Mythology

Key

C	Chthonic Characters
W	Women
H	Heroes
G	Groups
A	Antagonists
T	Transformations
DP	Dramatis Personae
PG	Primordial Gods
TW	The Trojan War
O	Olympians
TT	Titans

C — Chthonic Characters

Name	Symbol
Hades	H
Judges of the Underworld	Js
Persephone	P
Sisyphus	Sp
Cerberus	C
Hecate	Hc
Charon	Cr
Tantalus	Tn
Ixion	Ix
Thanatos	Th

W — Women

Name	Symbol
Pandora	Pn
Penelope	Pp
Amymone	Ay
Calypso	Cy
Nausicaa	Na
Ariadne	Ai
Atalanta	Al

H — Heroes

Name	Symbol
Orion	On
Orpheus	Or
Bellerophon	Bl
Jason	J
Heracles	Hk
Perseus	Pe

G — Groups

Name	Symbol
Fates	F
Muses	Mu
Furies	Fu
Hydra	Lh
Sirens	Sn
Daphne	Dh
Pyramus & Thisbe	Px

A — Antagonists

Name	Symbol
Cyclops	Cs
Chimera	Cm
Charybdis	Cd
Scylla	Sy
Medusa	Ms
Minotaur	M
Python	Py
Harpies	Hr
Circe	Cc
Atlas	Aa
Ganymede	Gy
Io	Io
Actaeon	Ac
Niobe	Nb
Pygmalion	Pg
Cassandra	Ca
Xenes	X
Iphigenia	Ih
Nesoi	Ns

T — Transformations

Name	Symbol
Echo & Narcissus	En
Callisto	Cl
Deucalion	Du
Baucis & Philemon	Bp
Leucippus	Le
Tiresias	Tr
Creon	Cn
Arachne	S
Iphis	Ip
Lysistrata	Ly
Prometheus	Pm
Hermaphroditus	Hd

DP — Dramatis Personae

Name	Symbol
Oedipus	Oe
Antigone	Ag
Agamemnon	Am
Electra	Ec
Clytemnestra	Ct
Andromache	Ad
Creon	Cn
Dionysus	Dy
Medea	Md
Aion	Ao
Ophion	Op
Hemera	Hm

PG — Primordial Gods

Name	Symbol
Chaos	Xx
Gaia	G
Ouranos	Ou
Pontus	Pu
Erebus	Eb
Nyx	Nx
Eros	Er
Chronos	Ch
Himeros	Ho
Thalassa	Tl

TW — The Trojan War

Name	Symbol
Paris	Pa
Hecuba	Hu
Menelaus	Ml
Priam	Pr
Helen	H
Odysseus	Oy
Hector	Hh
Aeneas	As
Ajax	Ai
Patroclus	Pr
Achilles	Ll

O — Olympians

Name	Symbol
Zeus	Z
Poseidon	Po
Athena	A
Artemis	At
Aphrodite	Ah
Hermes	He
Hera	Ha
Demeter	Dm
Apollo	Ap
Ares	Ar
Hephaestus	Hp
Hestia	Hs

TT — Titans

Name	Symbol
Cronos	T
Crius	Ci
Hyperion	Hy
Iapetus	Ia
Coeus	Co
Oceanus	Oc
Theia	Ta
Themis	Te
Mnemosyne	Mn
Phoebe	Ph
Rhea	Rh
Tethys	Ty

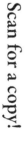

1

Chthonic Characters

To be Chthonic was to be of the underworld.

Hades, the realm of the dead which takes its name from its king, was a complicated place. It housed the three destinations for the spirits of the dead: Tartarus, for those to be punished, Elysium for those who had led heroic lives, and the meadows of Asphodel, for those who, like you or I, fall somewhere in between these two extremes.

Five rivers flowed through the underworld, too. Cocytus was a river of lamentation and mourning; Acheron – a real river in Greece – was known as a river of woe, found near the entrance to the underworld; Phelgethon was a river of fire encircling the region; and the Lethe was the river of forgetting – to drink from it was to forget your earthly life – a blessing or a curse?

Finally, the most famous of all the underworld rivers was the Styx, across which Charon ferried the spirits of the dead.

The ancient Greeks called their gods of the underworld *theoi khthonioi*, or "Chthonic" gods. However, while Hades, Persophone, and Hecate are undoubtedly deities, it would be wrong to call the whole of this group Chthonic Gods: the underworld was filled with figures who, while otherworldly, were not altogether godly...

After departing Charon's boat, spirits walked on, passing Cerberus, the three-headed guard-dog of the realm of the dead, before coming to the three judges who would decide on their spirit's final destination.

Most spirits were given their sentence by the judges of the Underworld, before settling to an eternity in one of the three regions of the dead, unless they were one of the small band of men who completed a katabasis – a journey out of the underworld. Only the likes of Heracles, Theseus, Orpheus and a small number of others managed it.

The Greeks understood that it was not normal to both enter the house of the dead and return to the land of the living.

2

Hades (H)

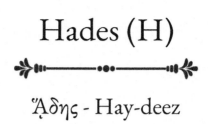

Ἅδης - Hay-deez

LIKE HIS YOUNGER BROTHERS Zeus and Poseidon, Hades ruled over a third of the *cosmos,* receiving the underworld (with which he shared his name) as his realm. Unlike his siblings, Hades was not one of the 12 Olympians but a Chthonic[1] god. The origin of Hades' name may relate to him as 'the unseen one', an attribute reflected in his "cap", which turned the wearer invisible.

Hades appears in few myths since he rarely leaves his realm. Aside from the myth of Persephone's abduction (his wife and Queen of the underworld) for which Hades is most (in)famous, the god appears primarily in *catabatic*[2] narratives, reflecting his chief concern that the border between the lands of the living and dead remain firm.

Hades was not readily worshipped by the ancient Greeks, with only two notable exceptions: a temple at Elis (but even then this only opened once a year and only to the priest) and at Mt. Minthe near Pylos. It was via his alternate persona/name, Pluton,[3] that Hades was included in the cult initiation of the Eleusinian Mysteries[4].

It can be difficult to differentiate between Hades/Pluton in art, but he is generally presented as a bearded male (similar to Zeus) holding items such as a sceptre, cornucopia[5] or pomegranate.

The Roman equivalent of Hades-Pluton, known as Pluto or Dis, was generally more grim than his Greek counterpart. Despite modern portrayals of Hades equating him with the Devil/Satan, this was never the case in antiquity (although Hades-the-realm was used to refer to Sheol/Hell in Hebrew/Christian scriptures).

Hades lends his name to several scientific taxonomies for species that live exclusively underground such as the Croatian centipede Geophilus Hadesi or the parasitic "flower of Hades", found only in the North Island of New Zealand.

Joel Gordon

Judges of the Underworld (Js)

Μίνως, Ῥαδάμανθυς, Αἰακός My-nos / Mee-nos, Rad-aman-thus, Ay-ak-os / Eye-ak-os

IN THE DEPTHS OF Hades, three venerable judges—Minos and his brother Rhadamanthys from Crete, along with Aeacus of Aegina—held court, assessing the lives of the deceased and dispatching souls to their eternal abodes.

These judges shaped the afterlife's landscape. Virtuous heroes found solace in the Elysian Fields or the Isles of the Blessed. The irredeemably wicked, like Sisyphus, Tantalus, and Ixion, were punished in Tartarus. The great mass of humanity was consigned to the Asphodel Meadows, a realm of dreary mediocrity.

In one telling, Rhadamanthys tried the dead from Asia, and Aeacus the dead from Europe, while Minos cast a deciding vote. Aeacus was also depicted as gatekeeper to Hades alongside Cerberus.

Minos and Rhadamanthys, born of Zeus' non-consensual union with Europa, and Aeacus, the product of Zeus' similar liaison with Aegina, had been earthly lawgivers and culture heroes. Minos was Zeus' only student and the author of wise laws forbidding drinking to intoxication. When Heracles killed his music teacher Linus, he invoked a law of Rhadamanthys pardoning acts of self-defence and was acquitted. Aeacus, renowned for piety, had petitioned Zeus to populate Aegina by transforming ants into men and to end a crippling drought across Greece.

Plato, who knew that philosophers were destined for the Isles of the Blessed, said that both those standing for judgement and the judges themselves stood naked, so that soul could confront soul in perfect transparency. In Dante's Inferno, Minos acquires a tail, which he twines around the damned, each coil representing the circle of Hell to which they were condemned.

Gregory Rowe

L. Mack inv. & mod.   E. Lohbauer del. & lith.

Persephone (P)

Περσεφόνη | Per-sef-uh-nee

PERSEPHONE, SOMETIMES KNOWN AS Kore (which means 'maiden' or 'girl'), occupies a distinctive place in Greek mythology. As the daughter of Demeter, the goddess of agriculture, and Zeus, the king of gods, her story is both captivating and poignant, delving into the complexities of life, death, and renewal.

Persephone's tale begins innocuously amidst the meadows, where she gathers flowers with her nymph companions. Her life takes a dark turn when Hades, the god of the Underworld, bursts out of the ground in his chariot, seizes her, and carries her to his realm. Despite her desperate cries, she becomes the queen of the Underworld, wed to Hades in an unsettling twist of fate. This abduction narrative, prevalent in ancient texts and rituals like the Eleusinian Mysteries, casts Persephone as both an aggrieved maiden and a powerful queen.

Pindar, the renowned poet, immortalised Persephone in his odes, talking of her 'ancient grief'. The exact nature of this grief remains elusive, revolving around her abduction by Hades or the tragic fate of her son, Dionysus Zagreus, in Orphic tradition. Regardless, the devotion of worshippers in the afterlife underscores Persephone's unique influence, allowing her to shape the destinies of the departed souls.

Persephone's significance extends beyond mythological narratives; she embodies the changing seasons; when she descends to the Underworld, nature withers, and life retreats as her mother mourns her loss. Conversely, her return heralds spring's arrival, bringing forth vibrant life – a perpetual cycle reflecting her own journey between the realms. Persephone's legacy reminds us of the interconnectedness of life, death, and renewal, prompting contemplation on the profound mysteries of existence.

The pomegranate, often associated with Persephone, remains a symbol of fertility and renewal across various cultures, reflecting her enduring influence on the concepts of life and rebirth.

Dr. Ellie Mackin Roberts

8

67

Inclyta diuinæ Cereris sum filia, raptam
Olim quam siculæ multum fleuere puellæ

5

Sisyphus (Sp)

❖⊪⊪————••••————⊪❖

Σίσυφος | Sisi-fuss

T HE FIRST KING OF Ephyra[1], Sisyphus was known as a cruel and crafty ruler who would kill guests and travellers in his home, violating the sacred principle of *xenia*[2] which angered Zeus. He also plotted – unsuccessfully – to kill his own brother Salmoneus, king of Salmone. After Zeus had abducted and hid the nymph Aegina, Sisyphus sealed his fate by betraying her location to her father Asopus.

In some versions of his myth, Sisyphus cheated death, further angering the gods. As Sisyphus was being chained in Tartarus[3] by Hades for his crimes, he tricked Hades by asking for a demonstration of the chains, trapping the god, thus preventing anyone on Earth from dying. In another version, Sisyphus told Persephone that he didn't belong in Tartarus and convinced her to release him.

Because of his hubris[4] and numerous offences to the gods, Sisyphus was condemned to the depths of Tartarus. Once re-captured, his punishment was to push a boulder, enchanted by Hades, up a steep hill for eternity, only for it to inevitably come crashing to the bottom each time.

Many thinkers have interpreted Sisyphus' punishment in different ways.

The philosopher Albert Camus wrote that Sisyphus is a metaphor for modern life, accepting ceaseless, meaningless, and absurd toil. The ancient Roman philosopher Lucretius saw Sisyphus' punishment as a symbol of the unending scramble for political power. For many ancient Greeks, the tale of Sisyphus was simply a lesson never to defy the gods.

Riley Gombis

A. Diepenbeeck fe.

Sisiphe

— ὁ μὲν χερσίν τε ποσίν τε
Λᾶαν ἄνω ὤθεσκε ποτὶ λόφον. ἀλλ' ὅτε μέλλοι
Ἄκρον ὑπερβαλέειν, τότ' ἀποςρέψασκε κραταῖῒς.
Αὖτις ἔπειτα πέδονδε κυλίνδετο λᾶας ἀναιδής.

Homer. Odyſſ. XI.

6

Cerberus (C)

Κέρβερος | Sir-ber-os / Ker-ber-os

CERBERUS, ALSO REFERRED TO as the Hound of Hades, was known to the ancient Greeks as the three-headed guard dog of the underworld. His role was to prevent those who had entered Hades from leaving. Anyone who attempted to leave risked being eaten by him.

Although Cerberus is usually described as having three heads, he is also shown in the ancient world to have as many as fifty heads, or as few as one head. He is occasionally depicted as having multiple backs, lion's claws, or even a mane of snakes and a serpent's tail. In most depictions, he wears a chain around his neck.

Cerberus comes from a family of creatures who share his characteristics of being both snakelike and multi-headed. His parents are the giant Typhon and the woman Echidna, both of whom are half-snake. His multi-headed siblings include the two-headed dog, Orthros, the nine-headed water serpent, Hydra Lernaia, and the three-headed Chimera.

Within mythology, Cerberus is commonly associated with the labours of Heracles. As his twelfth labour, Heracles was tasked by Eurystheus to capture Cerberus. With no weapons, Heracles managed to force Cerberus into submission and brought him back to Eurystheus, but he was eventually returned to the underworld.

Cerberus is also commonly associated with the myths of Orpheus and Eurydice, and the Aeneid, both of which involve Cerberus being put to sleep, allowing the living mortals to enter Hades. Within the myth of Orpheus and Eurydice, Orpheus puts the hound to sleep by singing to him. In the Aeneid, he is put to sleep with drugged honey cakes.

Modern depictions of Cerberus include his appearance in the Disney film Hercules, his short cameo within the song 'Surface Pressure' from Encanto, and as a loving pet in the video game Hades.

Brendon Little

7

Hecate (Hc)

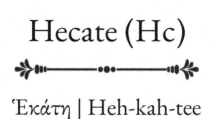

Ἑκάτη | Heh-kah-tee

H ECATE, A MYSTERIOUS AND enigmatic figure in Greek mythology, was the goddess of crossroads, witchcraft, magic and necromancy. Her parents were the great Titans Perses and Asteria, from whom she received her powers over heaven, earth, and sea. Hecate's origins are somewhat obscure, and she does not have the same level of comprehensive mythology as some other Greek gods. Nevertheless, her influence is undeniable.

Hecate is frequently depicted as a triple goddess, representing the stages of a woman's life: the maiden, mother, and crone. As the goddess of the crossroads, she held the power to guide travellers and assist them in making choices. This association with crossroads also extended to her role as a guardian of entrances, particularly those leading into the underworld. In Greek art and literature, Hecate is often linked to the night, the moon, and the spirits of the dead. She was revered in various rituals and ceremonies, particularly those involving magic and necromancy. Hecate was believed to have the ability to grant or withhold her favour in these practices, making her a powerful and feared deity.

Hecate's role in Greek mythology is multifaceted. She played a significant part in the story of Demeter and Persephone, helping Demeter search for her abducted daughter. Hecate also had connections to other deities, including Artemis, with whom she shared associations with the moon.

In later times, particularly during the Hellenistic and Roman periods[1], Hecate's significance in magic and witchcraft grew. She became a patroness of witches and a symbol of supernatural powers. Her image was often invoked in protective rituals and spells, emphasising her dual nature as both a benevolent and malevolent force.

In essence, Hecate remains a captivating figure in Greek mythology, embodying the mysteries of the night, the magic of the crossroads, and the power of transformation. Her influence has transcended the boundaries of ancient Greece, continuing to intrigue those who seek to understand the complexities of the mystical and the supernatural.

Zara A. Naveed

8

Charon (Cr)

❖━━━━━━━━━━━❖

Χάρων Kai-ron | / Cha-ruhn / Cah-ron

EVERY CULTURE HAS ITS own *psychopomp* – a fancy word for any sort of creature who guides the souls of the dead to their final destination. You may already be familiar with the ancient Egyptian jackal-headed god Anubis or the famous Valkyries of the Norse. In recent Western tradition angels have played this role. For the ancient Greeks, it was the legendary Charon who ferried souls to the realm of the dead.

Not an Olympian god, but something older, Charon was the son of the primordial Erebus and Nyx – Darkness and Night. Known as The Ferryman of the Dead, his role was to safely transport souls upon his skiff, across the River Acheron and to the realm of Hades.

Although he is never a central figure, instead featuring in the stories of others, Charon was incredibly important to the people of ancient Greece. Their dead were buried, entombed or cremated with Charon's obol[1] in order to ensure his services. If Charon was not paid this fee, a soul would be doomed to shiver on the banks of the Acheron, forever haunting the living as a ghost.

For gods and heroes this was less of an issue. During the *katabasis*[2] of his twelfth labour, Heracles simply intimidated Charon into giving him free passage. Orpheus charmed his way out of payment with a song. On separate occasions Odysseus and Theseus were clever enough to trick him.

Ancient Greeks depicted Charon on their urns as a withered old man. He appears in the epic Roman poem the *Aeneid,* portrayed with eyes of fire. You can find him in Renaissance art – famously in Michelangelo's *The Last Judgement* and even today there is still more than a shade of Charon in the Grim Reaper.ad

Craig Melia

And, lo! toward us in a bark
Comes on an old man, hoary white with eld,
Crying, "Woe to you, wicked spirits!"

Canto III., lines 76-78.

9

Tantalus (Tn)

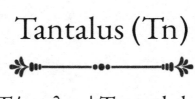

Τάνταλος | Tan-tuh-lus

Tantalus, king of Sipylus[1], was the son of Zeus and the nymph Plouto. He was married to Dione, and together they had three children: a daughter named Niobe, and two sons named Pelops and Broteas.

Tantalus was often a guest at the banquets on Mount Olympus[2], although he didn't always behave. On one occasion he stole the ambrosia and nectar of the gods[3], possibly in the hope of gaining immortality himself. Zeus was beside himself, but this was just the start of Tantalus' transgressions.

Wishing to test the gods' power of omnipotence, Tantalus committed one of the most shocking crimes in all of Greek mythology. He killed his own son, Pelops, chopped him up, cooked him in a stew and invited the gods round for dinner. All the gods except Demeter realised what Tantalus had done. Broken-hearted due to her daughter Persepone's abduction by Hades, she absentmindedly ate a chunk of Pelops' shoulder.

A furious Zeus ordered the Fates to resurrect Pelops and put him back together. They did this by re-cooking him in a magical cauldron but he was missing the shoulder Demeter had eaten, so Hephaestus fashioned a prosthetic one made from ivory.

Tantalus had committed a horrendous crime and his punishment was to be eternal suffering. Zeus sent him to Tartarus, the deepest region of the underworld. Here he stood in a pool of water and above him were branches of a fruit tree. Every time Tantalus went for a drink to quench his thirst, the water would recede out of reach. Every time he reached for the fruit to satisfy his hunger, these too were just out of reach.

The punishment of Tantalus gives us our word 'tantalising' – something which we want, but is just out of reach.

Matthew Speight

Ixion (Ix)

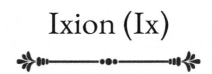

Ἰξίων | Ick-see-on / Ick-say-on

IN GREEK AND ROMAN mythology, Ixion was the king of the Lapiths[1]. He served as an example of the most severe punishments the gods could give for unjust behaviour, and is often named as authors describe the main sights of the Underworld.

After promising to pay a great dowry for Eioneus' daughter Dia, Ixion failed to pay the price after the wedding. In retaliation, Eioneus stole some of Ixion's prized horses. When Ixion discovered what Eioneus had done, he invited Eioneus over to settle the dispute; however, when Eioneus arrived, Ixion pushed him into a pit of fire, killing him. The crime of familicide and the violation of *xenia* were considered so vile that everyone refused to perform the rituals that would cleanse Ixion of his treachery and madness.

Watching Ixion live in exile and disgrace, Zeus took pity on him, inviting him to visit Olympus to feast with the gods. When Ixion saw Hera, he lusted after her and determined to sleep with her, further violating the guest-host relationship the Greeks valued so highly. When Zeus discovered his intentions, he crafted Hera's form out of the clouds and named it Nephele. Ixion slept with her, believing her to be Hera, and boasted about his success. Enraged, Zeus struck Ixion with the thunderbolt and cast him out of Olympus; Hermes was ordered to bind Ixion to a flaming wheel that would forever spin, stopping for a moment only at the sound of Orpheus' song as he bargained with Hades for the life of his wife Eurydice.

From the encounter between Ixion and Nephele resulted a child, Centauros, who established the race of centaurs. The Centauromachy[2], depicted on the Parthenon metopes, shows the battle that occurred when the centaurs attempted to kidnap Ixion's son Pirithous's bride on their wedding day.

Jenna Glassburner

CVI SIBI COR PRVRIT PLAVDENS POPVLARIBVS AVRIS.

PRO IVNONE SVA SVPPOSVIT NEBVLAM.

QVEM FAME STOLIDVM GLORIA VANA IVVAT.

ATRAM IVPPITER CVI IXION EI SIT EXEMPLO.

G. Cornelÿ Victor. fecit.

Hẽ. fecit 4.

43

11

Thanatos (Th)

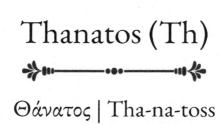

Θάνατος | *Tha-na-toss*

THANATOS WAS KNOWN AS the lieutenant of Hades, son to Nyx (night) and Erebus (darkness), brother to Hypnos (sleep), and the personification of death. With such a foreboding resume, Thanatos wasn't the first God on the altar in most Greek homes. He was looked on uncomfortably and barely spoken of, as death was a looming yet distant concept that Greeks wanted to avoid, until the moment he arrived at their doorstep. Many believed that when he came knocking, you were going to be dragged violently to the gates of the underworld to meet his colleagues of death. Tragically, however, he actually embodied a peaceful death, which his reputation masked quite well.

Despite his duties keeping him busy, Thanatos is also known for his quarrels with demigods and devious kings. After King Sisyphus of Corinth played with fire by interfering in immortal business, Thanatos was sent to chain him in his inescapable charmed shackles. Sisyphus, a lover of games, managed to trick death, who in turn shackled himself. This imprisonment meant that no death occurred until he was freed. Thanatos did eventually get his second chance with Sisyphus, in which he finally succeeded.

As if this wasn't enough, Thanatos also stepped into the ring with the demigod Hercules, son of Zeus, for the life of Alcestis, wife of Admetos. A match which he lost, therefore letting Alcestis return to the world of the living with extra time.

In our modern era, Thanatos' name and likeness has been leant to many characters in language, literature and cinema. Look no further than Thanos, the Marvel character responsible for the death of 5 trillion lifeforms in his story. Furthermore, with the image of death in mind, we often think of the Grim Reaper, a cloaked being, who carries a scythe and chains, to bring one to the afterlife. Finally, and more simply, we use the term Thanatophobia to mean the fear of death.

Lucy Elizabeth Farnan

Fig. 5.—*Thanatos.*

Women

I N ANCIENT ATHENS, WOMEN were considered by men to be little more than possessions – items belonging to the *oikos* (household). They had no political rights, and were restricted in how much they could leave their own homes – only being permitted to visit female neighbours. Their primary role was to bear children; the second was to weave cloth for their household.

The women of Greek mythology very often were only featured in stories connected with men, but despite being relegated like this, these characters have become some of the best known, and best loved..

Mortal women in Greek myth often had to endure the unwelcome (and occasionally welcome) attentions of mortal men or immortal gods. Their lives are often redirected by their encounters with the men and deities they meet, and seldom for the better.

Thankfully, new interpretations of these myths are restoring balance and giving voices to these women, and continuing the tradition of retelling, embellishing and reinventing the original source material.

Pandora (Pn)

❦⊷⊷—•••—⊷⊷❦

Πανδώρα | Pan-dor-ah

PANDORA WAS THE FIRST woman, according to the ancient Greeks, and she owes her creation to an act of vengeance. Angered by Prometheus sharing the secret of fire with mankind, Zeus assembled a crack team of Olympians to give men 'an evil thing in which they may all be glad of heart whilst they embrace their own destruction.'[1] This was to be Pandora.

Hephaestus moulded her exterior to be that of a beautiful girl. Athena taught her needlework. Aphrodite gave her a cruel longing and Hermes' contribution was 'a shameless mind and a deceitful nature.' Their creation was then dressed real pretty and sent as a gift to Prometheus' brother, Epimetheus. Epimetheus had been warned by his brother never to accept gifts from the Olympian gods, but had forgotten his brother's advice and took Pandora as his wife. It was whilst living with Epimetheus that Pandora came across the famous jar and thoughtlessly opened it.

Inside that jar was all the sickness and toil, along with sorrow and mischief that mankind had so far been free from. Left in the jar, after all the evils that hurt mankind had poofed out the window, was hope. It had got stuck under the rim.

Pandora's legacy was stark for mortals and set the tone for relations between Greek men and Greek women. "From her is the race of women and female kind ... who live amongst mortal men to their great trouble, no helpmates in hateful poverty but only in wealth."

Despite what you might think Pandora never had a box, it was always a jar. The box came about due to a translation error in the 16th century.

L.J. Trafford

LA BOÊTE DE PANDORE.

Pandora's Box.

Die Büchſe der Pandora.

De Doos van Pandora.

14

Penelope (Pp)

❧━━━━━━━━━━━❧

Πηνελόπεια | Pen-eh-lo-pee

SINCE ANCIENT TIMES, PENELOPE has been lauded as an "ideal" wife. Known for her loyalty and wisdom, she is often contrasted with her infamous cousins: Helen, whose adultery began the Trojan War, and Clytemnestra, who murdered her husband on his return.

The daughter of Icarius, King of Sparta, Penelope was wed to Odysseus after he won her in a footrace[1]. Taken to Ithaca as his queen, she gave birth to a son, Telemachus. He was only a baby when Odysseus sailed for Troy, leaving Penelope to guard the island in his absence. As the years passed suitors began to gather, but despite her father's insistence she refused to remarry.

With 108 men in her palace, eating her food and destroying her son's inheritance, Penelope turned to her loom. Promising to marry when she'd made a shroud for her father-in-law, she wove by day and unpicked the work by night. This fooled the suitors for three years, until she was betrayed by her slave-girl Melantho and forced to finish.

It's therefore fitting that Penelope's main epithet[2] is περίφρων (períphrōn), which is often translated as "wise" but literally means "to think around".

She even displayed this cunning against Odysseus, proving herself a match for him. When he returned, she feared it might be a trick, so rather than risk her fidelity she offered to move their marriage bed. Odysseus himself had carved it from an olive tree, and his anger at her suggestion proved his identity, allowing them to reunite at last.

Penelope's story is retold in works such as Margaret Atwood's *Penelopiad* and Claire North's *Ithaca*.

Naomi Rebis

Chantrey inv.

15

Amymone (Ay)

Ἀμυμώνη | A-mim-oh-nee

A MYMONE WAS ONE OF the Danaides, the fifty daughters of King Danaus. The king had originally led his family out of Libya to settle in the Peloponnese at Argos, but the land was suffering from drought and so Danaus sent his daughters out to find water.

While searching, Amymone came across a deer. Upon throwing a spear, she mistakenly struck a sleeping satyr who, now roused awake, attempted to rape her. Fleeing, Amymone called on Poseidon who heard her prayer, came to her aid, and killed the satyr. After making love, Poseidon led Amymone to the wells of Lerna and from their union was born the hero Nauplios.[1]

An alternative version of the story told how Amymone, having fallen asleep while searching for water, was rudely awoken by a satyr, who again wished to ravish her. Again, she invoked Poseidon to help her and he cast his trident at the brutish satyr. This time the god missed his target, instead striking a rock. However, Poseidon told Amymone to draw out the trident and when she did, a threefold spring now rushed forth. This was afterwards called the well of Amymone, as was the river for which it acted as tributary.[2] In this way, Amymone rescued the Argive Kingdom by ending its drought.

Some-time later, Danaus' twin brother, Aigyptos, sent his fifty sons to Argos in order to marry the Danaides, forcing the King to agree.

Yet the Danaides plotted with their father, and murdered their prospective husbands on the wedding night. Amymone herself slew Enceladus and buried his head at Lerna.

The Danaides are first mentioned by Hesiod in the 7th century BC, while Amymone's meeting with Poseidon was the subject of a satyr play by Aeschylus.

Ben Cassell

16

Calypso (Cy)

❧ﷻ———•❀•———ﷻ❧

Καλυψώ | Kah-lip-soh

ELUSIVE, SEDUCTIVE, DANGEROUS YET sympathetic, Calypso embodies many of the qualities that ancient Greek men feared in women. A sea nymph who resided on the island of Ogygia (the location of which was disputed by ancient authors) Calypso's story is imbued with a sense of the exotic. Much like the island where she spent her days cut off from civilisation, she is a figure surrounded in mystery. Even her name originated from the ancient Greek word καλύπτω (*kalyptō*), meaning "to conceal" or "to hide". Like many powerful women from ancient Greek mythology, Calypso was of divine descent. Daughter of the Titan Atlas, she held godlike powers in her abilities to seduce, persuade, and detain.

In Homer's *Odyssey*, the titular hero spent seven years in Calypso's company. Calypso's loneliness and desire for a companion drove her to charm Odysseus' mind; making him forget his home, encouraging him to stay. Despite her attempts to prevent Odysseus leaving, which included promising him immortality, their time together was marked by Odysseus' suffering, and longing for his family. It is likely that a Greek reader would have regarded her as a malevolent presence, using her voice as a weapon to corrupt a man renowned for his supposed loyalty to his family. Yet she is shown to also be just as powerless as mortal women who, like her, weave at their looms – a task symbolic of domestic order and female subservience.

Calypso's ability to strike fear and pity into the hearts of Greek men has endured over thousands of years. She has since been reclaimed as a feminist icon, who typifies the ambiguous role of women throughout history. She is now seen as powerful because of, not despite, her femininity. But perhaps her defining quality, her mysteriousness, means that she will continue to be reanalysed and reinterpreted for millennia.

Oliver Maynard

CALYPSOS ABSCHIED VON ODYSSEUS.

Druck & Verlag von Dr E. Albert, München.

17

Nausicaa (Na)

❖ ┉┉┉┉ •••• ┉┉┉┉ ❖

Ναυσικάα | Naw-si-kay-ah / Now-si-kay-ah

NAUSICAA, THE PHAEACIAN PRINCESS, was the daughter of King Alcinous and Queen Arete. Along with her parents and five brothers, she lived on the island of Scheria, the land of the Phaeacian people, which was where Odysseus arrived after his shipwreck (at the end of Book 5 in Homer's *Odyssey*).

The princess is described as being as fair and as lovely as the goddesses, especially Artemis. In her interactions with other characters, she is presented as both an intelligent and a charming young woman. It is clear that, at the time of Odysseus' arrival on the island, Nausicaa was considering marriage and preparing to find a suitable husband.

In the *Odyssey*, the goddess Athena disguised herself as one of Nausicaa's closest friends and visited the princess in a dream, instructing her to take the family washing to the river mouth. Nausicaa obeyed and, taking her maids with her, she drove a wagon down to the washing spot. As the girls were waiting for the washing to dry, they played with a ball and their shouts woke the exhausted Odysseus. While her maids ran away in fear at the sight of the wild-looking stranger, Nausicaa – with a little help from Athena – stood her ground and promised to help him, giving him food and clothing. She then showed him the way into the city, and told him exactly how to behave when given an audience with her parents.

Nausicaa does think about marrying Odysseus, and her father was willing to agree to such a union, but he had to bid farewell to the princess and return home to his wife in Ithaca. Nausicaa asked Odysseus to remember her forever as he owes her his life.

According to a later story, Nausicaa married Telemachus, Odysseus' son, and they had a child called Perseptolis.

Dr. Kerry Phelan

Nausicaa ayant rencontré Ulysse sur le bord du fleuve, elle le mène dans le palais du roi Alcinous son père.

18

Ariadne (Ai)

Ἀριάδνη | Ar-ee-ad-nee

T O THE ANCIENT GREEKS, Ariadne embodied intelligence, resourcefulness and resilience. Associated with mazes and labyrinths, her story intertwines with that of the gods and heroes through her associations with both Theseus and Dionysus.

Hailing from the island of Crete, Ariadne was born from a divine lineage, the daughter of King Minos, son of Zeus, and Pasiphaë, daughter of Helios. Ariadne was sister to Phaedra and half-sister to the Minotaur, the part-man and part-bull offspring of Pasiphaë and a sacrificial bull sent by Poseidon who was confined within a labyrinthine prison due to his monstrous appearance.

Ariadne's most famous role is her part in Theseus's legendary quest to conquer the Minotaur. Ariadne falls in love with Theseus and to aid him in navigating the complex labyrinth, she provides him with a simple but ingenious solution: a ball of thread. Theseus was to unravel the thread as he ventured into the labyrinth, allowing him to find his way back out after defeating the Minotaur.

Ariadne's story takes a cruel turn when Theseus, after his victory, abandons her on the island of Naxos whilst she is sleeping. This act of betrayal by the man whom she loved and betrayed her family for, leads to her discovery by the god Dionysus who immediately falls in love with her. Ariadne's marriage union with Dionysus sees her transformation from abandoned princess to divine being.

Ariadne continues to be a popular figure in the modern world, with 'Ariadne's Thread' being used to describe a complex puzzle, and her character and story being a popular inspiration in art, opera, poetry, music and literature.

As a wedding gift, Dionysus placed Ariadne's bridal crown in the heavens, where it formed the beautiful circular constellation we know today as the Corona Borealis, or the Northern Crown.

Lucy Angel

Angelica Kauffman Pinxit.

G. S. & I. G. Facius Sculpsit.

John Boydell excudit 1778.

ARIADNE awaked from Sleep, finds herself abandoned by THESEUS.

Published May 1st 1778 by John Boydell Engraver in Cheapside London.

19

Atalanta (Al)

―――◆❀||―――――•❀•――――――||❀◆―――

Ἀταλάντη | At-uh-lan-tuh

ATALANTA IS THE ONLY female heroine in Greek mythology with the same level of prestige as heroes like Heracles, Perseus, and Achilles. She is the only female to adventure with Jason and the Argonauts to retrieve the Golden Fleece. Her name is derived from *atalantos*, "equal in weight," suggesting that she was equal to men and referencing her ability to best men in contests.

The story goes that Atalanta's father was disappointed that she was born a girl rather than a boy, and "exposed" her to the elements.[1] Rather than dying, however, Atalanta was found by a bear who suckled and raised her to hunt and fight until she was eventually taken in by followers of the goddess Artemis, who taught her to use a bow and arrow. Atalanta became a skilled huntress and vowed to preserve her virginity.

Atalanta is famous for her involvement in taking down the Calydonian Boar that had been ravaging the region as punishment for the king's impiety against Artemis. The king's son Meleager fell for Atalanta and insisted she join the hunt despite the protests of men. She struck the boar allowing Meleager to kill it, but he credited Atalanta for the first strike that allowed him to do so.

Word of Atalanta's victory in the boar hunt reached her father, who decided to reclaim his daughter and propose that she marry and bear children. She agreed on the condition that a suitor had to beat her in a footrace. Hippomenes accepted the challenge, beat her (with the help of Aphrodite), and married Atalanta. They were eventually turned into lions for "desecrating" Cybele's temple.[2]

You can find Atalanta in the movie *Hercules* (2014), in TV series like *Hercules: the Legendary Journeys* (1995-1999), in the Hallmark miniseries *Jason and the Argonauts* (2000), and in the *Incredible Hulk* comics.

Dr. Christina Hotalen

Atalanta and Hippomanes, from an Original Drawing of B. Luti.

London, Pub.ᵈ March 10. 1791. by Ios.ᵖʰ Read, Coventry Court, Coventry Street.

20

Heroes

MANY OF THE HEROES we see today in films, games, comics, and TV come from archetypes set by the ancient Greeks and their tales of broad muscular strongmen, or wily quick-footed strategists.

They have endured in part because of popular admiration for their valour, courage, and strength, but perhaps even more so today for their foibles, their flaws, their failings, and fragility.

To be a Homeric hero was to be talented in war, and to be aided by the gods. Yet, all of these heroes – many of whom are today considered much less heroic than in the past – are made human by the qualities they *don't* have. Like all of us, they are a mix of talent and deficiency, but their achievements – immortalised in stories and songs – raise them far above the ordinary.

21

Orion (On)

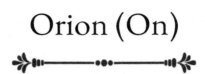

Ὠρίων | Uh-rye-uhn / Oh-rye-uhn

ORION WAS A HUNTER of giants and considered a hero in Greek mythology. Famed for his many love affairs, hunting prowess, and ultimately, his transfiguration into a constellation befitting his stature and good looks. Throughout antiquity, the constellation of Orion was responsible for guiding many travellers, and was known to the earliest Greek writers such as Homer and Hesiod.[1]

The myths surrounding Orion's parentage vary and are often contradictory. In some legends, he is the son of Poseidon and Euryale, daughter of King Minos of Crete. In another more dramatic story, the gods Zeus, Hermes, and Poseidon give King Hyrieus of Boeotia his greatest desire – a son. In either story, the presence of Poseidon gives an explanation for Orion's ability to walk on water and god-like stature.

The cause of Orion's untimely demise is also surrounded by mystery. In one instance he boasted he could kill every animal on Earth, drawing the attention of Gaia. Upset at his threats, she sent a scorpion to kill the hubristic hero with a poisonous sting. Another tale lays blame on the god Apollo. Jealous of Artemis' relationship with fellow hunter Orion, he challenged his sister to test her archery skills aiming across a vast lake at a bobbing object. Unbeknownst to Artemis, the target was Orion swimming, and in mourning her beloved companion she had him immortalised as a constellation.

What is conclusive in all accounts is that after his death Orion was placed among the stars, most commonly identified by his belt – a trio of bright stars in a straight line. Joined in the heavens by several other constellations; alongside him, his faithful hunting dogs Canis Major and Canis Minor;[2] the Pleiades,[3] and pursued by Scorpio, the scorpion.

Whenever Scorpio appears in the sky Orion hides away. Perhaps this lends weight to the scorpion being responsible for this hero's untimely end.

Ciara Meehan

22

Orpheus (Or)

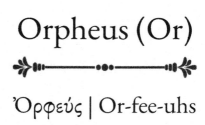

Ὀρφεύς | Or-fee-uhs

MANY ARTISTIC LIVES HAVE been spent appealing to the world's masses, but perhaps no one has been as masterful as Orpheus in this pursuit. Ancient Greek authors could fathom no greater poet or musician than Orpheus, whose talent was so irresistible that no person was immune to his charm.

Orpheus' mythological parentage is contested (Thracian king Oeagrus and Apollo are potential fathers, and sisters Calliope and Polymnia are among the potential mothers), but Orpheus is dubbed "the father of songs" without argument. Orpheus is the namesake for the Orphism religion. His successful descent to – and return from – the Underworld, joined him with Dionysus and Persephone, whose reverence is rooted in journeys of a similar nature.

This Underworld trip is the focal point of Orpheus' legacy, less for his return than for who was left behind. Orpheus descended to rescue his beloved Eurydice, who'd been fatally snakebitten. Hades and Persephone were moved by Orpheus' music enough to let Eurydice return on the condition that Orpheus lead the journey back to the upper world and not look back until the pair were both back where they'd started. Infamously, Orpheus turned in excitement as he completed his journey, breaching his pact and causing Eurydice to fall back into death.

Representations of Orpheus are plentiful. Criterion Collection includes many films invoking him, including Jean Cocteau's *Orpheus* (1950) and *Testament of Orpheus* (1959) as well as Marcel Camus' *Black Orpheus* (1959). In 2022, *Sight and Sound* ranked Céline Sciamma's *Portrait of a Lady on Fire* (2019), a film reliant on the narrative of Eurydice's death, number 30 on its list of the greatest films ever. Players of the video game *Hades* (2021) can interact with Orpheus, helping to pen a new chapter in a mythology that's yet to get old.

Mike Delayo

23

Bellerophon (Bl)

❧·❦━━━━━·❦·━━━━━❦·❧

Βελλεροφῶν | Buh-leh-ruh-fon / Bell-eh-ruh-fon

BELLEROPHON (ALSO CALLED BELLEROPHONTES) was born to Eurynome, wife of Glaucus of Ephyre (Corinth), and sired by Poseidon. Glaucus was the son of Sisyphus, and, like his father, incurred the ire of the gods, in his case by feeding his horses human flesh to make them "stronger." He suffered an "untimely fall" from his chariot and was devoured by his bloodthirsty horses.

Bellerophon never believed in his divine parentage until a revelation in the Temple of Athena. He'd gone there seeking help in taming Pegasus, the winged steed born from Medusa's wellspring. His prayer was answered; in a vision, Athena gave him a golden bridle, and he awoke to find it miraculously at his side. He tamed Pegasus, and lived in Ephyre until he accidentally murdered his brother.

Exiled to Argos, he sought the king Proteus's purification for fratricide and stayed many weeks. One night, Bellerophon rejected the queen Anteia's romantic advances; the next day, she told the king that Bellerophon had tried to force himself on her. The king was furious. He couldn't kill Bellerophon for the sake of *xenia*, but sent him off with an unsealed letter to Iobates, King of Lycia, telling him to immediately kill the letter's bearer. But Iobates dined with Bellerophon before reading the letter, binding himself to xenia also.

Instead, he sets Bellerophon on an impossible task: to kill the Chimera, a lion with the tail of a snake's head, and a fire breathing goat's head on its back. Bellerophon killed the Chimera by flying over its flames and shooting it with arrows. He also defeated other Lycian "problems" before hubristically attempting to fly to Mount Olympus to join the gods. Zeus sent a gadfly to sting Pegasus, who flung Bellerophon off its back before joining Zeus' stable. Bellerophon, impaired from his fall, died alone disgraced before gods and men.

Chris McGonigle

FLEXIBVS ALIGERI DELVSA, ET CVSPIDE FIXA,   CONCIDET HÆRESEOS RABIES: DELAPSAQVE CÆLO
P. P. Rub. VT CECIDIT MAGNO SVB BELLEROPHONTE CHIMÆRA,   VNANIMES TANDEM IVNGET CONCORDIA BELGAS.   F. a T. sc
inu.   HAVD SECVS INVICTO FERNANDI ROBORE, DIRA

C. Geuat.

24

Jason (J)

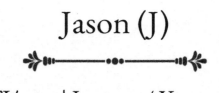

Ἰάσων | Jay-sun / Yay-sun

J ASON IS, IN MANY ways, the least "heroic" of the Greek heroes. His abilities are distinctly human and he relies heavily on the superhuman abilities of those around him, with his own heroic journey never really working out for him.

Jason was the son of Aeson, the king of Iolcus who was overthrown by his half-brother Pelias. When Jason confronted Pelias, he was sent on a quest to Colchis[1] to retrieve the mythical Golden Fleece, the hide of a flying golden ram that was sacrificed there. Jason gathered many mythical heroes to join him on his ship, the *Argo*, including major figures in Greek mythology like Heracles, Orpheus, Castor and Pollux, Achilles' father Peleus, and (according to some sources) Atalanta.

Jason and the Argonauts set off on their journey, navigating many challenges to arrive in Colchis. Once there, the Colchian princess Medea used magic to assist Jason in performing several challenges for her father, the king Aeetes. Eventually the two stole the fleece and navigated their way back to Colchis, escaping the Sirens and defeating the bronze giant Talos in the process.

Yet Jason, ever the unheroic hero, was not successful in regaining the throne of his father. After Medea had tricked Pelias's daughters into killing him in the hopes that it would make him young again, Jason and Medea fled to Corinth, where Jason left Medea to marry the Corinthian princess. A spurned Medea then killed her and Jason's own two children before fleeing the city. Left alone and without the gods' favour, Jason died an unceremonious death, being crushed beneath the *Argo*, the very ship with which he had performed his great journey.

The 1963 film Jason and the Argonauts *was especially noteworthy for its combination of live-action and stop-motion animation, especially in Jason's battles with Talos and the skeleton warriors of Colchis.*

Aidan Scully

62. *Draconem velleris excubitorem sopit Iason.*

25

Heracles (Hk)

Ἡρακλῆς | Heh-ra-klees / Hair-a-klees

THE GREATEST (AND BEST-DOCUMENTED) of the Greek heroes, Heracles[1] was to the Greeks the quintessential warrior: an amazingly strong demigod[2], bearded, musclebound, and usually depicted cloaked in a lionskin and carrying a club. He alone among demigods was transformed into a full god at his death. He was worshipped and invoked[3] for many centuries and his adventures were a favourite subject of visual artists of the fifth and sixth centuries BCE.

Heracles was born in Thebes to Alcmene, a mortal woman for whom the god Zeus lusted. He visited her one night disguised as her husband Amphitryon while he was away and Heracles was conceived. Everyone noticed right away that he was an exceptionally strong baby and so must be of divine origin, but Amphitryon raised him as his own son alongside his mortal twin brother Iphicles.

His heroic exploits began when Hera, upset over her husband Zeus' infidelity, sent two serpents to kill the baby in his cradle and he strangled them instead. From then on, Hera was one step behind the hero. In one notorious episode she drove him temporarily insane and he murdered his young sons thinking they were enemies.

In penance for this abominable act, Heracles undertook his famous twelve labours. The Nemean lion with its impenetrable hide, he killed with his bare hands. The head-sprouting Lernean hydra he cauterised at the neck as he chopped off its many heads, smashing its one immortal head beneath a boulder. He tamed the savage Cerberus, three-headed guard dog of Hades. The labours were often acts of service to human communities who were suffering under the tyranny of monsters, but in the end they justified his ascendance to godhood as well.

A task is said to be 'herculean' when it is extremely difficult and daunting.

Christina Osborn

26

Perseus (Pe)

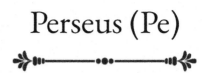

Περσεύς | Per-see-yus / Puh-say-uss

Perseus was one of the greatest heroes of Greek mythology, most famous for slaying the gorgon[1], Medusa. He was the son of Zeus and Danae – the daughter of Acrisius, the King of Argos.

Acrisius, who was disturbed by a prophecy that he would be killed by the son of his daughter, imprisoned Danae. Zeus visited her in a shower of gold leaving her pregnant despite the king's best efforts. Fearing the wrath of the gods, Acrisius decided not to kill the child directly, and instead ordered Danae and Perseus to be thrown into the sea in a wooden chest.

The chest was found by the fisherman, Dictys, who raised Perseus on the island of Seriphos. Dicty's brother was the scheming king, Polydectes, who fell in love with Danae. Perseus wanted to protect his mother from Polydectes and agreed to a dangerous quest to bring the king the head of Medusa.

Perseus prayed to Athena who told him to seek out the Hesperides[2] for help without telling him how to find them. To track them down, Perseus forced the three Graeae[3] to give him the location by snatching the one eye they shared.

The Hesperides gave Perseus a sack for Medusa's head and other gifts from the Gods, including the winged sandals of Hermes, a cap of invisibility from Hades, a sword from Zeus, and a polished shield from Athena.

Perseus found Medusa in the Gorgons' cave and used her reflection on the shield to cut off her head. On his return journey Perseus rescued Andromeda[4] from the sea monster Cetus by using the head. Perseus returned to Seriphos and saved his mother from Polydectes by turning Medusa's head on the king. Later on, Perseus competed in games by throwing a discus. Perseus' throw hit and killed a spectator – his grandfather, Acrisius.

Herodotus, the ancient Greek historian, believed that the Persians traced their lineage to the son of Perseus and Andromeda, Perses.

Peter Wright

41. *Anguiparum Medusæ caput præscindit Perseus.*

Groups

❧≡———•••———≡❧

F ROM TIME TO TIME several characters are found in these stories who are inseparable from one other. Here, we have three such groupings: the Muses, the Erinyes (the Furies) and the Moirai (the Fates).

Each of these groups had individual and collective responsibilities, interacting with the mortal world, shaping destinies, and sometimes ending them.

The Muses were goddesses of the arts, including astronomy, but have been inspirational for all areas of human endeavour. It is perhaps appropriate that their mother was Mnemosyne, the Titan of memory, as it is through repetition over time that their creations have survived.

The Iliad explains that the Erinyes "take vengeance on men" and these Tartarean goddesses exact their anger through violence against the spirits of those doomed to eternal punishment. Greek religion did not promise happiness in the afterlife, and belief in these avenging goddesses may have encouraged good behaviour in their mortal believers.

A human life-span was determined by the Moirai, who represent our mortality and the finite nature of our time. They are reminders that we must make the most of life, before it is cut short.

Fates (F)

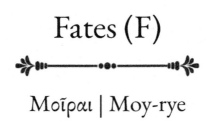

Μοῖραι | Moy-rye

THE FATES WERE THREE daughters of Nyx. They determined the destinies of every mortal; Klotho the spinner spun the thread of life at the point of birth, Lakhesis the allotter measured the thread to determine how long and happy a life the mortal would receive, and Atropos the inflexible cut the thread to end that life. As such, the Fates decided birth, death and everything in between. Plato says that the sisters sang, with Lakhesis singing of events past, Klotho of the present, and Atropos singing of events yet to occur, for they were all-knowing. Their decisions were final and unchangeable, and even the gods dared not interfere.

Hubris, though, didn't stop some from trying to change their fate...

When Meleager was born, the Fates visited his mother, Queen Althaea of Kalydon. Klotho announced that the boy would be noble, Lakhesis declared he would be courageous, but Atropos foretold that he would die as soon as the log on the hearth was burnt up. Althaea hastily put out the fire and hid the log, thinking that son would be safe as long as only she knew the prophecy.

However, years later Meleager killed his uncles during the Kalydonian boar hunt when they insulted his beloved Atalanta. Out of her mind with grief, furious Althaea avenged her brothers by retrieving the log and casting it into the fire. As the log disintegrated into embers, Meleager collapsed and died, and to her horror Althaea realised that the Relentless Ones were inescapable, and had always known this would come to pass. She hanged herself out of sorrow.

The Greeks called them the Moirai, while the Romans called them the Fatae or Parcae. Gladiators in Greece and Asia Minor[1] still called them by their Greek name; on their gravestones they explain that they died in the arena because the Moirai snipped their threads.

Alexandra Sills

29

Muses (Mu)

❧❧━━━━•••━━━━❧❧

Μοῦσαι | Myoo-ziz

THE MUSES WERE THE nine[1] ancient Greek goddesses of the arts and sciences. Born to Zeus and Mnemosyne, they were thought to be the source of creative inspiration and purveyors of knowledge that was passed down by the Greeks through centuries of oral tradition[2]. Many ancient authors began their poems, plays, hymns, and histories with an invocation to the Muses, calling on them to help, or to use the author as a vessel for their song.

Spending their days singing and dancing on the slopes of Mount Helicon, the Muses each presided over a specific creative pursuit and were sometimes depicted with an identifying attribute. Melpomene, for example, as the muse of tragedy, would often be shown holding a tragic mask or knife. There was also Calliope, the muse of epic poetry; Clio, history; Erato, love poetry; Euterpe, lyric poetry; Thalia, comedy; Polyhymnia, religious hymns; Urania, astronomy; and Terpsichore, choral song and dance.

Often accompanied by Apollo, one of the Muses' main roles in mythology was performing at Olympian celebrations or the funerals of heroes. They could also be found judging and participating in musical contests, though the outcome was usually tragic for any mortals who challenged them; blinded, stripped of their abilities, even transformed into magpies for presuming their skills could match a muse.

These goddesses have been capturing imaginations for as long as humanity has loved to create and discover. Shakespeare's invocation in the prologue of *Henry V*[3], the rock band MUSE, and the narrators of Disney's *Hercules* are just a few examples. We even see their influence in words like 'museum' and 'music' (which both evolved from Greek *mousa* 'muse'), as well as the nickname many artists give to their inspiration, 'muses'.

The lyric poet Sappho was hailed a 'tenth muse', because she was so admired in the ancient Greek world and beyond.

Lorna Lee

ОУРАΝΙΑ   ΘΑΛΕΙΑ   ΕΥΤΕΡΠΗ ΠΟΛΥΜΝΙΑ ΤΕΡΠΣΙΧΟΡΗ ΜΕΛΠΟΜΕΝΗ   ΕΡΑΤΩ   ΚΛΕΙΩ   ΚΑΛΛΙΟΠΗ

Point par Jules Romain.   Dessiné par J. B. Wicar.   et Gravé par Marais.

APOLLON ET LES MUSES.

30

The Furies (Fu)

Ἐρινύες | Fyur-ees

VENGEFUL MONSTERS OR HARBINGERS of justice, the furies were known by many names throughout the Classical period. The serpent-haired Erinyes of Hesiod's *Theogony*, the vengeful Eumenides of Aeschylus' *Oresteia* and the three monstrous Furiae of Virgil's *Aeneid*.

As Chthonic deities, the Erinyes are associated with the earth and the underworld, punishing the souls of Tartarus and ascending to earth to pursue the sinful. Some attribute their parentage to Hades and Persephone, others to the goddess Nyx. According to Hesiod, they sprang from the blood-soaked earth following the castration of Uranus by his son, the Titan Cronus. The nature of their conception ties them to concerns of familial crimes, seeking vengeance for offences committed against kin, particularly parents.

They are most notably associated with the pursuit of Orestes following the murder of his mother, Clytemnestra. The tale is famously dramatised by the tragedian Aeschylus, in which they acquire a new role as protectors of justice, known as the benevolent Eumenides or "kindly ones", a euphemism used in fear of calling the dreaded deities by their name.

When summoned from the underworld by a curse or the breaking of a blood oath, the fearsome Erinyes are said to have inflicted madness, unbearable guilt, blindness and disease upon their victims. Relentless in their pursuit, inflicting famine on towns and punishment on those who harbour their targets.

Typically dressed in black chitons, with a menacing demeanour and bloodshot eyes, they are the very personification of vengeance. They are just as terrifying in appearance as they are in their capabilities, appearing throughout ancient literature and art as winged, serpent-haired monsters, carrying whips and torches. By the time they emerge as Furiae in Virgil's *Aeneid* standardised as three sisters: Tisiphone, Alecto, and Megaera, they are confined to the underworld, overseeing the punishment of the wicked.

Ashley Ann Cassidy

37. *Iunonis ad Furias alloquium.*

31

Antagonists

I T IS HARD TO deny that very often, we are rooting for the bad guy. We know they're the villain, and that they're up to no good, but we are drawn to them anyway.

The ancient Greeks knew how to put together a good bad guy, too. They provide the foil against which the hero must struggle, and in doing so they bring out the heroic qualities of the hero. Without Polyphemus the Cyclops, for example, Odysseus is much less of a hero.

Time has been kind to some of these characters, and as our own society's attitudes have changed, so has our attitude to the villains. It is rare to see any of these characters now as purely evil, and perhaps this is due to a deeper understanding today that people who do bad things are not necessarily evil, and their behaviour may have been prompted by a horrific backstory (or a really annoying hero).

Whatever our feelings towards them, these antagonists are some of the most complex figures in any mythology, helping us to ponder the important question: what is it that makes someone bad?

32

Cyclopes (Cs)

❦⊱━━━━━━⊰❦⊱━━━━━━⊰❦

Κύκλωπες | Sy-clo-pees / Sy-clops / Kee-clop-ees

SEVERAL SPECIES OF DWARF elephants[1] inhabited various islands on the Mediterranean during the Pleistocene period, just before the advent of our species. Their skulls, vaguely similar to that of a human's – with a gaping hole for the trunk reminiscent of a solitary eye socket – were probably among the chief origins of the legends behind the Cyclopes.

The Cyclopes are first mentioned in the works of Hesiod, as some of the monstrous children born from the union of Gaia and Uranus. Their name means "circle-eyed", since... "a single circle-shaped eye was set in their foreheads".

Homer also mentioned them in the Odyssey, as a race of barbarians without agriculture, arts, or law, "each a lawgiver unto himself" ... He was also notably unclear on whether they had one eye, or two.

Later on, Euripides also wrote a play named *Cyclops*, where he located these "one-eyed sons of Poseidon" in Sicily, dwelling in remote caves. Euripides also credited them with building 'cyclopean' masonry; heaven-high walls "fitted snug with red plumbline and mason's hammer..." Many other authors throughout the Hellenistic and Roman eras referred to these monstrous beings.

Throughout antiquity, pre-existing works of large, irregular stone masonry around the Mediterranean were often termed "cyclopean", harkening back to this mythical race in a curious association between ancient relics and non-human intelligence – a theme which continues in fringe beliefs and conspiracy theories in the present day.

According to Callimachus, the cyclopes also built the bows and arrows that were later used by Apollo and Artemis.

Cevdet Mehmet Kosemen

EX ARCHE.
TYPO PALEATI
BRIXIENSIS

Cum Privilegio

Cornelio cort ft

33

Medusa (Ms)

❧┉———••••———┅❧

Μέδουσα | Meh-joo-suh / Me-dew-sah

IN THE GREEK MYTHS, Medusa was one of the three gorgon sisters born of the marine deities, the sibling-couple Phorcys and Keto. The physical depiction of Medusa and her sisters – Stheno and Euryale – has varied considerably over time. Widely agreed upon is a humanoid woman with monstrous hair constructed of venomous snakes, and eyes that can turn the living into stone with a single, unobstructed look. Medusa is however, known for her mortal death at the hands of the son of Zeus, the demi-god Perseus.

Instructed by Polydectes[1] to retrieve the head of Medusa, Perseus was assisted by Athena, who guided Perseus as he located Medusa in the reflection of a bronze shield, and Hermes, who provided the sickle Perseus used to behead the gorgon. From the newly severed remains of Medusa emerged the winged horse Pegasus, and the humanoid Crysaor. Perseus then used the decapitated head of Medusa to turn Polydectes (and others) to stone. The head of Medusa was in turn gifted to Athena to decorate her aegis[2].

Medusa was not always considered an ugly monster throughout antiquity. Ovid instead tells a variation of the story where Medusa is human-born; a beautiful and chaste mortal priestess of Minerva (Athena) who was sought after by Neptune (Poseidon) and raped by him inside a shrine to Minerva. Minerva, supposedly offended by this, subsequently transforms Medusa into her commonly known appearance. The Ovidian retelling of events has more recently been adopted by modern feminist movements – reinterpreting this Greek "monster" as a victim of the patriarchy, a powerful icon for sexual assault survivors, and/or viewing the actions of Minerva not as a punishment, but as a gift to Medusa to provide some protection for herself after her ordeal.

To be petrified with fear, means literally to be scared into stillness, like a statue. This word comes from the Latin petra: rock.

Tyler-Jade Kelly

Tête de Méduse de la coupe Farnèse, au Musée de Naples. — Dessin de Sellier.

34

Circe (Cc)

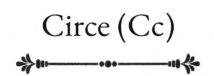

Κίρκη | Sur-see / Keer-kay

CIRCE, KNOWN TO THE ancient Greeks as a fair-locked goddess and a powerful sorceress, dwelled on the mythical island of Aeaea. She was skilled in the magical arts of potioncraft and necromancy, and possessed the power to turn humans into animals. Her specialty was transforming her enemies into pigs. With a group of lions and wolves for her companions, Circe lived and worked on her secluded island, weaving at her loom and crafting elixirs, until she was interrupted by a group of men on a long journey home.

As a daughter of the Titan Helios, Circe was a member of an illustrious family of immortals. Her father was the sun, dragging his golden chariot through the sky each day. Her mother, Perse was a daughter of Oceanus, the gargantuan river encircling the world. Circe's siblings were skilled in magic and rulers of their own territories.

Circe was well known to the ancients for her role in assisting Odysseus on his journey home from the Trojan War. When the men had survived their encounter with the Laistrygonians[1], they landed upon the shores of Aeaea. After an unpleasant introduction involving men transformed into pigs, Odysseus managed to win Circe's affection, and her invaluable help with completing his quest. Circe supplied him with the information he sought, and sent him away after one year of rest. Many depictions of Circe can be found in art and literature, and she is often a feared and respected figure.

Circe's name comes from the Greek verb kirkoô, *meaning "to hoop around", referencing the power of magic to bind or secure a person or thing into another form.*

Baily D. Peters

135. *Ulyſsis ſocij a Circe in porcos.*

35

Atlas (Aa)

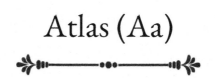

Ἄτλας | At-lass / At-luhs

ATLAS WAS ONE OF the Titans, the son of the Titan Iapetus and the Oceanid Clymene (or Asia). He had brothers who were noteworthy in Greek mythology, including Epimetheus, Menoetius, and Prometheus.

After the Titans were defeated in the Titanomachy[1], they were imprisoned in Tartarus. However, as Atlas was one of the leaders during the war, Zeus had a special punishment for him. He was condemned to stand at the western edge of the Earth and hold the celestial sphere (the heavens or the sky) on his shoulders for all eternity. In other mythology, he holds the pillars which separate the Earth and the sky. This punishment of carrying the celestial sphere is the most recognised illustration of Atlas and has been a significant image in art, literature, and popular culture.

One of Heracles' twelve labours was to retrieve the golden apples of the Hesperides (Atlas' daughters). Heracles needed Atlas' help to retrieve the golden apples and Atlas agreed to help him if he took on his burden, hoping to trick him into taking this responsibility indefinitely. After Atlas returned with the apples, Heracles realised he was being deceived and asked Atlas to hold the heavens while he adjusted his cloak. When Atlas took the burden back, Heracles grabbed the golden apples and ran, leaving Atlas to carry the celestial sphere once again.

The next Greek hero to visit Atlas was Perseus. Perseus had asked Atlas for hospitality. However, Atlas had feared this was a trick, like Heracles, so turned him down. Perseus in a rage showed Atlas the head of the Gorgon, Medusa, which turned Atlas into stone.

This relates to Atlas' enduring legacy, as the mountain range in North Africa – the western edge of the ancient Greek world – are called the Atlas Mountains, after the myth with Perseus. Moreover, modern atlases are named after the Titan, with his geographical knowledge, and were first used in the 16th century.

Ryan Marc Williamson

36

Hydra (Lh)

❧ ⊷—•••—⊶ ❧

Ὕδρα | High-druh / Hee-druh

To the ancient Greeks, the Hydra was a formidable, serpentine monster that was often associated with fresh-water sources and subterranean rivers (*hydra* meaning 'water-serpent' in Greek). The Hydra was a scourge to the sacred springs of blessed Lerna[1] and dwelled near the source of the Amymone river. Hydra represents the more disturbing aspects of Greek mythology: a polluting monstrosity whose duplicitous many-heads were a threat even to the most vigilant of heroes.

Hydra was born to the baleful nymph Echidna and serpentine-giant Typhon, amidst a litter of similarly dreadful beasts.[2] Hydra is described as having an enormous, dog-like body, from which a legion of heads erupted. These heads were regenerative, in that, if one were decapitated, two more would take its place. Hydra's blood was also highly toxic, with those coming into contact with it suffering a slow, agonising death.[3]

Hera nurtured the Hydra in the Lernaean swamp, where it grew and terrorised the surrounding plains. For his Second Labour, Heracles was tasked with slaying the monster. Coaxing the creature from its lair, Heracles strained against both the serpent's endlessly regenerating heads, and an enormous crab which Hera had summoned to assist them. Smashing the crab beneath his foot, Heracles rallied and instructed his companion, Iolaus, to cauterise[4] the Hydra's severed heads with fire (preventing their regrowth). He then decapitated the immortal head and buried it beneath a rock.

The Hydra is one of the most recognisable creatures from Greek myth, with numerous depictions in books, video games and movies. Famously, the Hydra appeared as guardian to the Golden Fleece in the 1963 film *Jason and the Argonauts*.

'Hydra' is the name given to the largest of our constellations, because of its serpentine shape. The Crab (which assisted Hydra against Heracles) was rewarded for its courage and now forms the constellation 'Cancer'.

Connor Hickey

37

Chimera (Cm)

✦━∎∎∎━━━━●●●━━━━∎∎━✦

Χίμαιρα | Ky-meer-uh / Key-meer-ah / Chee-mee-rah / Kee-meh-rah

UNDIFFERENTIATED, UNMEASURABLE AND INDETERMINABLE, the Chimera defies all classification. It is the archetype of all that is fluid and in-between, of every body that resists. Homer tells us that the Chimera had the head of a lion, the back of a serpent, and the body of a goat in the middle, and Hesiod adds that it breathed fire and was of divine origin. But who is to say that this was *the* Chimera – that it wasn't a shapeshifter, or a hybrid being altogether beyond our understanding?

After all, the lineage of the Chimera is shrouded in mystery; perhaps it was born from Echidna, perhaps from Typhon, perhaps from no-one at all. Perhaps it has always been with us. Likewise, the location of the Chimera is mysterious; the ancients situated it in Lycia (that is, in present-day Turkey), but it was also entirely Greek in its appearances. Perhaps it is situated nowhere, in the cracks between our pavements, the niches between our classifications. Perhaps the Chimera dwells in the shadows, as they recede, between the world of our dreams and our so-called waking world; the edges of our maps; the uncharted terrain in our laboratories.

For the Chimera is still with us, and surrounds us every day. Homer says it was slain by Bellerophon, and Hesiod adds Pegasus to the mix, with the hero victorious over the creature in an air battle. But the idea of the Chimera lives on. Every day, Bellerophon's successors in biology, physics, and chemistry, in gender assignment and school assessment, in means-testing and insurance underwriting, attempt to slay the Chimera that resists classification. But every day the Chimera comes back, as bodies morph and mingle, figures dissolve and reconfigure, gestures unfold and unravel.

Sascha Engel

UBI ADSUM.   24.   VITIOSA ABSUNT.

38

Minotaur (M)

❧•••———•••———•••❧

Μινώταυρος | My-nuh-tor / Min-uh-tor

THE MINOTAUR (LITERALLY THE Bull of Minos) was a monster, half man and half bull, who lived in King Minos' Labyrinth near the palace of Knossos.

He was fed on human sacrifices – boys and girls who were sent by the people of Athens as a tribute. The Minotaur was particularly important to the Athenians because of his role in one of their foundation myths[1], the story of the cult hero[2] Theseus. Theseus volunteered to be one of the sacrificial youths. He killed the Minotaur and escaped the Labyrinth (with the help of the Cretan princess Ariadne), and returned home to become King of Athens.

The Minotaur wasn't just a monster. The Greeks gave him a family and a back-story. He was the child of Queen Pasiphae by the white bull of Poseidon, and was sometimes represented in art as a baby sitting on his mother's lap. King Minos, who imprisoned him, was his stepfather, and Ariadne, who gave Theseus the means to kill the Minotaur, was his half-sister. He was also the nephew of Circe and the cousin of Medea. He even had a name: Asterion or Asterius, meaning 'starry'.

The Minotaur is known for being unique. Unlike the hybrid races (the Centaurs, for instance, or the Harpies), there was only one Minotaur. Perhaps that is why his story comes up so often today in children's and young adult fiction: it's used to explore isolation and what it means to be different.

The oldest literary sources don't actually specify which half of the Minotaur was man and which half was bull, so artists through the ages have come up with some interesting interpretations!

Dr. Cora Beth Fraser

74. *Minotaurum Theseus vincit.*

39

Python (Py)

❧━━━━━━━━━❧

Πύθων | Pee-thon / Pie-thon

Python is a complex character in Greek myth. Whilst it was one of the most terrifying monsters, in death it brought about the creation of one of the key oracular sites[1] in the ancient Greek world.

In some variations of the myth, Python is one of the horrific children of Gaia and was born out of the mud.[2] The Python was thought to be a large creature most likely a serpent, with Menander Rhetor describing a creature covered in spirals and coils. Python is consistently described as living in or around the mountains near Delphi. As the omphalos of the world (literally meaning bellybutton!) Delphi held great spiritual significance for the ancient Greeks, and the myth of the Python is heavily interlinked with the overall mythos of the site. Some argue that the Python owned the site at Delphi, while others state that the Python was laying waste to the surrounding countryside. Regardless of which variant of this myth the Greeks held to be most accurate, the story of the Python ends with a confrontation with Apollo.

It is important to remember that the site of Delphi, Apollo, and the Python itself were all synonymous for the Ancient Greeks with oracles and prophecy. As the god of oracles and prophecy it may make logical sense that Apollo might want his own oracular centre. However, other stories have the Python pursuing Leto, the mother of the twins Apollo and Artemis, on the orders of an (unsurprisingly) jealous Hera. As Leto was carrying around the two babies, the infant Apollo somehow manages to murder the Python. Apollo then buries the Python under the omphalos, and sets up the oracular site. The vile fumes from the corpse were thought to aid the Pythia[3] in uttering forth their fabled prophetic visions.

Alice Main

13. *Immensum certis strauit Pythona sagittis*   *Latonę matri monstrum Junonis ob iram*
    Nec meruit minimum Cynthius arte decus,   *Et terra infestum dum necat atzẹ mari.*

40

Harpies (Hr)

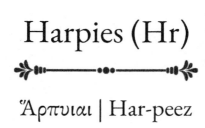

Ἅρπυιαι | Har-peez

Y OUR GRANNY HASN'T RETURNED from her morning visit to the Acropolis? A flock of Harpies snatched her. Your father is yet to return home after a full day at the agora[1]? Harpy. That bowl of soup you left cooling in the evening breeze which has suddenly disappeared? You guessed it – Harpies. So, who are these elusive fiends with a flair for kleptomania?

The most common depiction of a Harpy has been one of a bird of prey with the head of a gaunt, sinister woman. These wicked hybrids were a personification of intense winds, whose role was to pluck evildoers from Earth and take them to their reckoning in front of the Erinyes[2] – or sometimes straight to their eternal damnation in Tartarus – leaving nothing but chaos and deafening sounds in their midst. Although known as the Hounds of Zeus, Harpies also served Hades as one of the many monsters guarding the gates of the Underworld.

Appearing first in Homer's poems, there are many stories surrounding their roles as the Gods' vessel for the torture of mere mortals, their most notorious being the punishment of King Phineus of Thrace. Phineus, having been given the gift of prophecy by Apollo and following a common theme among mortal Kings in Greek mythology, misused his new power as a Seer, leading to his own demise. In true Zeus style, blinding Phineus simply wasn't punishment enough, he was also sent to a remote island where he was damned to sit, starving for eternity, in front of a bountiful feast, only to have any food snatched away from his mouth by a ravenous flock of Harpies. Thus, the Harpies' image as the ancient Greek equivalent to the modern-day, food-thieving, utterly fearless, and savage seagull was born.

It is interesting to note that the harrowing stories of Harpies as fearsome female creatures that were once so feared by men has withstood the ages, from their presence in Homer, to the seventh circle of Dante's Inferno, only for the word "harpy"[3] to be so casually used as a 21st century misogynist insult, employed to try and undermine female power.

Alisha Dodds

41

Sirens (Sn)

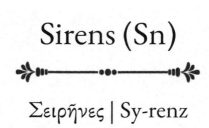

Σειρῆνες | Sy-renz

Sirens are infamous for their seductive song, which lures those who hear it to their doom. They're usually depicted as women, and in Greek mythology, they're portrayed with both humanoid and avian[1] features. How many of them there are, what their names are, and which island they live on varies by source material.

Originally, the sirens were handmaidens of the goddess Persephone before she was taken down to the Underworld by Hades. Demeter transformed them into bird-like creatures to aid them in their search for Persephone.

Many heroes encounter the sirens on their voyages. The Argonauts almost fell prey to them; they're only saved because Medea instructed Orpheus to play loudly and sweetly enough to drown out the sound of the sirens' voices. Only one man, Butes, was affected by the song, and he jumped overboard and swam towards the sharp rocks of the island. However, Aphrodite took pity on him, and he was saved from a grisly death.

Odysseus and his crew also passed by the isle of the sirens, though they were forewarned by the witch Circe. His crew stopped their ears with wax, but Odysseus wanted to hear the song. His crew tied him to the mast of the ship, and the sirens tempted him with songs promising wisdom and knowledge as he sailed past.

Sirens have been conflated with mermaids since the medieval period. Very few contemporary depictions of sirens have any avian characteristics; instead, they have tails and scales, though they retain their bloodthirsty nature. Many works of fiction feature sirens, such as the Young Adult novels *To Kill A Kingdom* by Alexandra Christo and *A Song Below Water* by Bethany C. Morrow.

The inventor of the siren alarm named his creation after the sirens of Greek mythology since his contraption could produce sound even under water.

Megan Mahoney

50. *Sirenes Proserpinæ comites in aues.*

Transformations

TRANSFORMATION IS AT THE centre of Greek mythology. It is so central, that the Roman poet Ovid wrote a whole collection of them in the first century BCE, called *Metamorphoses*.

These are stories of gods turning themselves into animals and humans; and of humans being transformed into animals, monsters, flowers, and stars.

Some of these myths helped Greek society to conjure explanations for how the world came to exist in its current shape, and answer enduring questions such as "where did the first spider come from?" and "why are mulberries red?" Often, in the absence of scientific knowledge, myth fills the gap.

Other tales of transformation experimented with taboo subjects: murder, incest, and other transgressive behaviours. These stories provided both a moral precedent and a way of speaking about the unspeakable.

Most importantly, transformations were explosions of imagination, providing inspiration for artists, writers, scientists, and musicians for thousands of years. These stories resonate because they ask us to entertain two important inquiries: what are we, and how would it be if we were something else? Drawing us to these questions, we are encouraged to be open-minded, and from there we find empathy and compassion.

Scylla (Sy)

Σκύλλα | Si-llah / Ski-lah

SCYLLA WAS ONE OF two dangers faced by the ancient Greeks when they sailed through a narrow strait between mainland Italy and Sicily, the other being Charybdis. Scylla was a sea monster who preyed upon sailors whose boats came close to the cliffs where she resided. At times she is described as having twelve legs and six heads on long necks which she used to pluck sailors from their boats with her sharp teeth. On Greek vases, Scylla appears as a beautiful woman with a long fish tail and dog heads sprouting from her waist. Homer describes her voice as sounding like the yelping of a young puppy.e

Scylla was once a beautiful naiad[1] who was transformed into a monster by a potion poured into the water where she bathed. In one version of the story she was loved by Poseidon and the poison was administered by Amphitrite. Hyginus describes that Glaucus was in love with Skylla, Circe transformed her into a monster because of jealousy.

Scylla represented the dangers of maritime travel. In myths, sailors faced a choice between losing their entire ship to Charybdis or losing some of their crew to Scylla. In the Odyssey, Scylla took six of Odysseus's men and Odysseus prayed to Scylla's mother, Crataeis, that his ship would only be attacked once as they passed by. Jason and the Argonauts, Aeneas, and Heracles all faced the dilemma of facing Scylla or Charybdis – Aeneas made a different choice by avoiding the Strait of Messina and sailing around Sicily instead.

'Between Scylla and Charybdis' is an idiom that means having to choose between two different, but awful options.

Lauren Murphy

Moreau inv.   Helman Sculp

44

Charybdis (C)

❧⊷———•••———⊶❧

Χάρυβδις | Kah-rib-diss

THE ANCIENT GREEKS UNDERSTOOD Charybdis to be a monstrous, ship-and-sailor devouring, whirlpool. She lived, if one can say a whirlpool *lives*, below a cliff where there grew a large fig tree that disguised the danger beneath. Three times a day, Charybdis would swirl and suck the sea around her down to the sea floor, destroying everything in her path, before reversing to spit the remnants back out.

There are only ancient theories as to Charybdis' origins and parentage. Even whether or not she was believed to be a sentient being who could have parents, rather than some natural phenomena, is uncertain. If she had parents, they were likely primordial deities of the sea, or the sea and the earth themselves.

Charybdis didn't work alone in her torment of ships and sailors. She existed alongside the monstrous creature Scylla who lived across the narrow strait where Charybdis swirled. The pair's earliest and most famous devouring is found in Homer's *Odyssey*, where Odysseus narrowly escapes the pair, twice (his crew was not so lucky!). The only way to successfully pass through the strait was to be attacked by either Charybdis or Scylla. Since passing Charybdis meant the loss of one's ship, sacrificing a few sailors to Scylla was the safer choice. It was better to lose a few men to the many jaws of Scylla, than to lose one's entire ship and its crew to Charybdis. This worked for Odysseus once, but the second time he faced Charybdis his ship was pulled down into her waters, and only he survived by clinging to the tree above.

Charybdis became a common enemy to sailors, appearing in other stories of journeys across the sea including Apollonios' *Argonautika*, and later the Roman Virgil's *Aeneid*, who placed the real life location of Charybdis as the Strait of Messina.

Liv Albert

45

Echo and Narcissus (En)

Ἠχώ & Νάρκισσος | Eh-koh, Nar-siss-uss / Nar-kiss-us

THE STORY OF ECHO and Narcissus is centred around self-love and unrequited love. Both were from Boeotia, and said to be beautiful, with the gods Apollo and Pan pursuing Echo, and Narcissus' beauty being legendary.

Echo was a dryad[1] forced to repeat the last words of others by Hera. Echo distracted Hera with long, lavish tales, whilst Hera's husband Zeus pursued other dryads. In other versions of the tale, Echo lost her own voice entirely, only being able to repeat words in another person's voice.

Narcissus was born to the river god Cephissus and naiad Liriope. He grew up to be a hunter, and often stalked the woods in Boeotia.[2] The prophet Tiresias[3] claimed that Narcissus would live a long life, as long as he did not "know himself", meaning seeing his own reflection.

Echo stumbled upon Narcissus in the woods, instantly falling in love with his beauty. Narcissus heard her and called out "Who's there?", but she could only repeat him. Upon seeing her, Narcissus rejected Echo causing her to run off in her grief. In her pain she called out to the goddess of revenge Nemesis[4], who cursed Narcissus to fall in love with his own reflection. Unable to move or reach out to his reflection in the pool, he died wasting away by getting lost in his eyes and was transformed into a flower.

In death they both endured what cursed them in life; Narcissus stared at himself in Styx's pool[5], and the flower was revered as beautiful by the ancient Greeks. Echo's lack of self-love, meant she still loved him in death and pitied Narcissus as he faded away, echoing his "Farewell" to the world, back at him.[6]

The story is thought to be an explanation of the prophecy from Tiresias and is where the narcissus flower and Echo came from.

George McAdam-Cross

46

Ganymede (Gy)

❧——•••——❧

Γανυμήδης | Gan-ee-meed / Gan-ee-me-dee

I N THE PALACE OF lofty Olympus, a handsome Trojan prince dashed between the twelve gods, dutifully filling their cups to the brim. Known as Ganymede to the Greeks, and Catamitus to the Romans, this mortal-turned-immortal youth was the cupbearer of the gods, usually depicted with a Phrygian cap, a rooster, a hoop, or a lyre.[1]

Golden-haired Ganymede was one of the three sons of Tros, lord of the Trojans, from whom the city of Troy's name is derived. Due to being the loveliest of all the mortals, the youth inevitably caught the eye of the great sky father, Zeus. In some myths, Zeus sent his sacred bird, the eagle, down to bring Ganymede to Olympus to pour and serve ambrosia to all twelve Olympian gods. In other versions, it was love-struck Zeus himself who rushed down from the heavens in the guise of an eagle, desperate to have the beautiful prince as his own personal cupbearer and wine-pourer.

To compensate the grieving King Tros for the abduction of Ganymede, Zeus granted him the finest of horses, and sent Hermes to tell him that his son had now become deathless and unageing. Upon this news King Tros exchanged his mournful demeanour for joy, now knowing Ganymede had achieved immortality and eternal youth.

Ganymede's name was derived from the Greek words *ganumani* "gladdening" and *medeôn*, "prince" or "genitals" – possibly to deliberate a double-entendre. The Trojan prince became a companion and friend to Eros and the two were commonly portrayed playing games of contest or luck together. Ganymede was occasionally identified as a god of (homoerotic) love and desire.

Ganymede was often conflated with the constellation Aquarius, the star formation known as the "Water-Carrier" or "Cup-Bearer", which is also adjacent to the constellation Aquila, "the Eagle." One of Jupiter's Moons is also called Ganymede.

Tobias Fulton

47

Io (Io)

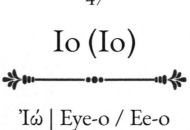

Ἰώ | Eye-o / Ee-o

Io WAS THE BELOVED daughter of the river god Inachus. Her lineage includes many famous heroes and kings of Greek mythology, including Perseus, Minos, and Heracles. Io represents many themes that were important to the Greeks in their stories, like transformation, divine infatuation, jealousy, and punishment and exile.

The beautiful Io caught Zeus's ever-wandering eye, leading him to pursue her and leave her father heartbroken at her kidnapping. Knowing his wife Hera would be angry at his infidelity, Zeus transformed her into a snow-white heifer. Hera saw through the ruse, claimed the heifer, and placed her under the 100-eyed monster Argus's guard. Io was distraught, trapped in her bovine form and unable to return to her father. To avert her fate, some stories say Zeus summoned Hermes the messenger god, others suggest it was Io's father Inachus who requested divine aid. In either case, swift-footed Hermes was requested to help bring Io back from Hera's clutches and save her from Argus.

Hermes put Argus to sleep with his lyre and killed him. Hera retaliated by sending a gadfly to torment Io, who wandered the earth in agony. Eventually she reached Egypt and pleaded with the heavens for mercy. Zeus persuaded Hera to relent, and he transformed Io back into a human. Finally free, Io married an Egyptian King, Telegonus and produced a royal lineage that would last many centuries.

The story of Io is referenced in many ancient sources including Ovid's *Metamorphoses* and Hesiod's *Theogony*. In 1610, the famous astronomer Galileo Galilei discovered Jupiter's four largest moons. He named them after famous lovers of Jupiter (Zeus' Roman equivalent). Io became one of these moons.

Amber Taylor

Eximia est Io specie decorata: sed ipsam
Jupiter amplexus cogit inire suos.

Postmodo quæ vultu induitur formáque juuencæ
A Ioue, dum coniunx imperiosa venit.

Ouid. Metamorph. libr. I.

Crispin van de Passe inuen. et exc.

Daphne (D)

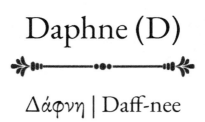

Δάφνη | Daff-nee

THE ANCIENT GREEKS HAD many different versions of Daphne's story. All generally agree that she was a nymph, and that her rejection of the god Apollo led to her transformation into a laurel tree. The earliest story, from the fourth century BCE, by the philosopher Palaephatus, describes her as a daughter of Mother Earth and attributes her refusal of Apollo to the philosophical concept of *sophrosyne,* or a healthy state of mind.

Two later Hellenistic authors, Diodorus of Elias and Filarcus of Athens, report a story in which Apollo pursues Daphne out of jealousy: Daphne, devoted to Artemis, has sworn off marriage, and so in order to pursue her, Leucippus disguises himself as a huntress to hunt with her. Apollo sees this, is inflamed with jealousy, and pursues Daphne himself. Zeus is responsible for her transformation in this story.

However, the most famous and well-known version of her myth comes not from the Greek world, but the Roman. The Latin poet Ovid includes Daphne and Apollo as one of the many myths of transformation in his *Metamorphoses.* In Ovid's version, Cupid, annoyed by Apollo's boasting about being the best archer, strikes Apollo with an arrow that makes him fall in love with Daphne, and Daphne with an arrow that makes her shun all romantic relationships. Apollo pursues her, and in desperation she asks her father, the river god Peneus, to save her. She is turned into a laurel tree, and Apollo declares that because she can't be his wife, she will be his tree, and crown the heads of all Roman victors as they enter Rome in Triumph.

Today, authors interested in retelling Daphne's story have tried to help her regain her agency, either by making her a fierce warrior or by having her fight back in tree form.

Alicia Matz

DAPHNE

PRIMVS AMOR PHŒBI DAPHNE PENEIA. OVID

49

Baucis and Philemon (Bp)

Βαῦκις & Φιλήμων | Baw-siss / Bow-kiss and Fee-lee-mon / Fill-eh-mon

THE TALE OF BAUCIS and Philemon appears only once, in Ovid's epic poem the *Metamorphoses*. Their story begins with Zeus and Hermes (Jupiter and Mercury to the Romans) walking the earth disguised as mortals. Seeking hospitality and shelter, they were faced again and again with barred doors and refusals – until, at last, they reached the rush-thatched hut where the elderly couple Baucis and Philemon dwelt.

Unlike their richer neighbours, Baucis and Philemon invited these strangers in and made them welcome in their humble home. Ovid dwells at length on the simplicity of their home, juxtaposed with the generosity with which this devoted couple offer up what little they have to their guests. In return for their generosity, Baucis and Philemon are spared the fate of their neighbours, destroyed in a great, god-given flood which drowns the surrounding area, turning the valley into a great lake. Their home is transformed from mud-brick to marble, turned into a temple to the gods. Baucis and Philemon are also granted a boon by Zeus himself.

Their wish was that neither should outlive the other, and be forced to mourn for their beloved spouse, but that they should both die at the same moment. Having lived out the rest of their years as faithful temple guardians, in their last hours both began to sprout leaves on their limbs. As their limbs became wooden and bark crept up their skin, they turned to each other and wished the other farewell until the bark closed over their faces and they were transformed. An oak and linden tree, still whispering to each other, stood over the doors of the temple – a monument to the hospitality of Baucis and Philemon.

Carys Hughes

Iupiter et fandi Deus hospitis ora ferentes   Bancidis est templum casa: vir, mulierq, senescunt
Urbibus exclusi rustica tecta petunt.   Arboris in ramos: morte, maloq̃ carent.

50

Deucalion (Du)

❧⊱━━━━⊰❧

Δευκαλίων | Dew-kay-lee-on

THE THIRD GENERATION OF humanity, built from clay by the divine brothers Prometheus and Epimetheus, were deeply flawed – they were lawless, violent, and refused to respect their gods. In his anger, Zeus decided to wipe the slate clean, and so sent a great flood across the world, destroying the failed generation of humanity.

The son of Prometheus, Deucalion, and his pious wife Pyrrha were warned of the coming disaster and instructed to build a chest to save them from the flood. They floated in the chest for nine days and nights. When they again reached land at Parnassus, they performed sacrificial rites to Zeus, who was soothed by their dedication to the gods. He sent Hermes to give them instructions: to take the 'bones of their mother' and throw them over their shoulders. Deucalion and Pyrrha took stones from the ground, the bones of their great mother Gaia, and from these stones grew the new generation of humans.

As a son of Prometheus, Deucalion was afforded a noble position among humanity – he ruled as the king of Phthia, a region of ancient Thessaly, and his legacy extended throughout all of Greece. Although the ancient sources give differing accounts of Deucalion and Pyrrha's children, many refer to his son, Hellen, as the progenitor of the entirety of the Greek race. Deucalion's grave is located in Athens, where he fled with his family after the flood, and there are also some ancient sources that credit Deucalion with the building of the Sanctuary of Olympian Zeus.

As a key player in the creation of humanity, Deucalion's legacy in the contemporary era rests in many science fiction and fantasy world-building elements. He lends his name, for example, to a werewolf antagonist in MTV's television adaptation of *Teen Wolf*, and as the title of a vampiric bloodline in the video game, *Vampire: The Requiem*.

Tanika Koosmen

12.

Diluuio cessante, et subsidentibus vndis
E saxis hominum gens reparata fuit

12.

Pyrrha nurus post terga iacit, post terga maritos
Deucalion, durum nos genus vnde sumus.

51

Callisto (Cl)

❖❖—••——••—••—❖❖

Καλλιστώ | Kuh-lis-tow

CALLISTO WAS A BEAUTIFUL nymph[1] in Greek and Roman mythology who followed Artemis, the virgin goddess of the hunt.

Zeus, king of the gods, became obsessed with Callisto's beauty and began pursuing her, but to be part of Artemis' girl-gang you had to reject the company of all men. Not one to relent, Zeus continued to scheme, and noticing the close relationship between Callisto and Artemis, he appeared in the form of the goddess. Believing she was being seduced by Artemis, Callisto willingly became intimate with Zeus.

Time passed, and it became clear that the nymph had become pregnant, and one day while she was bathing with Artemis, the goddess noticed her swollen stomach. Artemis was outraged, kicking Callisto out of her following, where she gives birth to a son, Arcas, alone.

Ancient sources disagree over who performs the transformation, but soon either a furious Artemis, or a jealous Hera (the wife of Zeus), turned Callisto into a bear in their anger.

Eventually Callisto in bear-form strayed too close to a group of hunters, and was pursued by her own son Arcas who, not recognising the bear as his mother, tried to shoot her. In the moment before the arrow hit, Zeus delivered her in an act of *catasterism*[2], placing her among the stars to live forever as the constellation Ursa Major or 'Great Bear'. Her son was immortalised as the 'Lesser Bear', or Ursa Minor.

Later receptions of this myth, particularly in paintings from the Renaissance period to the late 18th century, emphasised the homoeroticism of the narrative, frequently depicting the moment of intimacy between Callisto and the false Artemis.

The name Callisto comes from the Greek Kalliste (Καλλίστη), meaning 'most beautiful'.

Yentl Love

Martinus Ginsert
Saenredam sculp.

Cum privil. Sa. Ce. M.
1599

Dum dekrectanti Jovis vestis adempta est,
Celatum in nudo deprensum est corpore crimen.

Cornelius Schonjus.

52

Arachne (S)

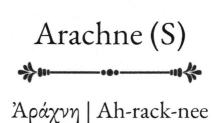

Ἀράχνη | Ah-rack-nee

Aᴄᴄᴏʀᴅɪɴɢ ᴛᴏ Oᴠɪᴅ's *Mᴇᴛᴀᴍᴏʀᴘʜᴏsᴇs*[1], Arachne was a Lydian[2] girl of humble origin whose talent for weaving and embroidery gained her fame across the region. Her technique was such that even the nymphs that lived nearby came regularly to watch her skill while working.

Her greatness led her to believe she was better than Athena, who was patron of various crafts, especially spinners and embroiderers. She even dared to challenge the goddess to a weaving contest. According to the myth, Athena disguised herself as an old lady, and tried to warn Arachne against comparing herself to the gods, without success, for Arachne replied only with mockery.

After such an offence, Athena threw off her disguise, beginning the contest. The goddess weaved a scene that praised the twelve Olympian gods, and four sequences in which mortals were punished for defiance. Meanwhile, Arachne portrayed some episodes of illicit affairs of the gods[3], with the clear intention of putting them to shame.

Once the competition was over, the goddess found herself unable to point to a single technical flaw in Arachne's work. Enraged by her skill and the defiance of exposing the wicked acts of the gods, she ripped the tapestry and crushed the girl's spirit. Arachne ran away, and in her shame she tried to hang herself. Athena took pity on the young girl and prevented her death, but ultimately transformed her into the first ever spider, condemning her and all her descendants to weave endlessly.

The myth of Arachne went on to be an origin myth for the existence of spiders, but was also clearly meant to be a cautionary tale about hubris. We can find the impact of this prideful young woman in almost every modern romance language, for spiders are all named after her[4].

Anna Fernández Iglesias

ARACHNE

Telarum inuentrix operosa obseruat Arachne 3 Stamina et aurato mutantem vellera luto
Leuia versatq ducentem Clostra suso, Ternaq arundinem quatientem licia dente

53

Actaeon (Ac)

᾽Ακταίων | Ack-tay-on / Ack-tee-on

ACTAEON WAS THE SON of Aristaeus and Autonoe, one of the daughters of Cadmus, the founder of the Greek city of Thebes. Thebes, as one of the oldest cities in the Greek world, features in many mythological stories including that of Oedipus. It was also the birthplace of Semele, the mother of the god Dionysus and another daughter of Cadmus.

Actaeon's fate was to be torn apart by his own hunting dogs. This horrible demise shares alarming similarities with that of Pentheus, the young king of Thebes, as told most vividly in Euripides' tragic drama *The Bacchae*. Pentheus' mother, Agave, was another daughter of Cadmus.

The accounts of why Actaeon was killed in this way vary: some accounts suggest that he was punished for his hubris when he rated himself a better hunter than the goddess Artemis. Others say that he had inadvertently caught sight of the goddess naked whilst she was bathing in a grove, and was punished for seeing what no mortal should ever see. In the best-known version of the tale by the Roman poet Ovid, he is transformed into a stag before he is killed.

The mythical narrative may seek to explain prohibitions on access to sacred places, or perhaps may in some way represent the religious ritual of animal sacrifice, with Actaeon representing the sacrificial beast, and the hounds the worshippers.

Later painters such as Veronese and Titian focussed not on the savage act of dismemberment but on the moment when the naked goddess is discovered (the painting of mythological nudes allowed painters to circumvent the prohibitions on pictorial nudity that were in place for renditions of biblical scenes).

Dr. Mike Beer

54

Pyramus and Thisbe (Px)

Πύραμος καὶ Θίσβη | Pir-ah-mus, Thiz-bee

To the ancient Greeks, the story of Pyramus and Thisbe was one of remaining faithful in love, even up to and beyond death.

Forbidden from getting involved with the girl next door, Babylonian teenager Pyramus might have been forgiven for having felt like his chances of love were hopeless. In fact, even though their houses were connected, his family was locked in a deadly rivalry with that of his beloved Thisbe. Things changed, though, when they found they could talk through a crack in the wall. They quickly professed their love and agreed to meet at a nearby mulberry tree by a tomb.

Arriving first, Thisbe surprised a lioness which had just finished dining on an ox, and immediately fled in such terror that she lost her cloak as she ran.

Her mouth still bloody from her meal, the beast tore the cloak to pieces and left it bloodstained on the ground. Pyramus was devastated when he reached the tomb to find the bloodied cloak surrounded by lion tracks – proof, surely, that Thisbe had been killed. There was nothing left for him to do but follow her into death by falling on his own sword. So violent was his death that his blood sprayed across the mulberry tree, staining its berries a dark purple. Thisbe returned to the scene a few moments later. Heartbroken, she prayed to the gods, to her parents, and even to the mulberry tree to allow her to be buried with her beloved – and killed herself with the same sword. The gods were moved by this and allowed the lovers to be honoured by turning the berries of the mulberry dark red from then on.

The most famous retelling of this story, of course, is Shakespeare's Romeo and Juliet, but it has been brought into the modern day by both The Beatles and The Simpsons.

For all the romance of its name, Britain's "Pyramus and Thisbe Club" exists to facilitate discussion of the legislation around shared walls between properties.

Ross McGovern

32. *Thisbe Pyrami exemplum æmulata pectus sibi transuerberat.*

55

Hermaphroditus (Hd)

Ἑρμαφρόδιτος | Her-maf-ro-dite-uss

HERMAPHRODITUS WAS A DEITY who had both male and female sexual characteristics, usually depicted as a penis and breasts[1]. They have been an important figure for both intersex and transgender people throughout history.

As their name suggests, Hermaphroditus was the child of the gods Hermes and Aphrodite. They were incredibly beautiful, and were often included in depictions with other love deities. In some versions of Hermaphroditus' story, they were born intersex, but in Ovid's version of the story, they are transformed.

In Ovid's Metamorphoses, the story goes that Hermaphroditus was born a man and raised by nymphs. One day whilst swimming in a pool they were found by the naiad Salmacis, who was an outcast amongst nymphs. Salmacis fell madly in love with Hermaphroditus, and begged them to be with her. Hermaphroditus, however, rejected her.

So, Salmacis waited for them to leave the pool and forced a kiss upon them, pleading with the gods to let them be together forever. The gods granted her wish, and the two became one with dual sexual characteristics. Hermaphroditus was so angry that they cursed the pool to transform any other man who bathed in it.

Despite this, Hermaphroditus symbolised for many Greeks and Romans the perfect union of male and female, and became associated with marriage. Due to their connection with nature, statues of them, often sleeping, became a popular feature in Roman gardens, with many paintings depicting intersex people in Pompeii!

The most famous statue of Hermaphroditus is now in the Louvre, but many people don't realise that the bed they are sleeping on is not ancient, but created by the Italian sculptor Bernini in 1620. The statue originally was sleeping on rocks! Ouch!

Evie Chandler

HERMAPHRODITE.

London Pub.d July 1 1787 by Torre & C.o N.o 132 Pall Mall

56

Leucippus (Le)

❧ ⦁⦁⦁ ————— ⦁⦁⦁ ————— ⦁⦁⦁ ❧

Λεύκιππος | Loo-sip-us / Loo-kip-us

L EUCIPPUS IS A RARELY mentioned character of Greek myth who undergoes social and later biological transition to live his life as a man. Our only Classical source for Leucippus is the 2nd/3rd century CE *Metamorphoses Synagoge* by Antoninus Liberalis.

Leucippus was born at Phaestus on Crete to Lamprus and Galatea[1]. Lamprus and Galatea were poor and this, together with other patriarchal and misogynistic trends in ancient Greece, led Lamprus to pray for a son and to order his pregnant wife to expose the child if a girl was born. Galatea went into labour while Lamprus was away tending his flocks, and she gave birth to a girl. Moved by pity for her newborn, Galatea decided to secretly raise their daughter as a boy. As puberty approached, it became impossible to maintain the deception, so Galatea prayed to Leto for assistance. Her prayers moved the goddess, who changed the sex of the child into a boy's.

The citizens of Phaestus commemorated this miracle by sacrificing to Leto in a festival called the Ecdysia or "the Stripping". This festival was a rite of passage for boys becoming men, who would first put on feminine clothing (*peploi*) and strip them off at the end. The association with boys as "unformed" men with women also hints at the generally misogynistic beliefs of the ancient Greeks.

Brides and bridal couples in Phaestus also developed a tradition of lying beside an image of Leucippus before their wedding, but Antoninus gives no explanation for this custom.

In modern discussions, Leucippus is often forgotten in favour of the more popular Iphis, with whose story that of Leucippus shares many elements. Unlike in the story of Iphis, however, we have no reference to Leucippus's feelings about this transformation.

Leucippus' home of Phaestus was the second-largest Minoan settlement after Knossos.

Samuel Azzopardi

57

Tiresias (Tr)

❧•ⅠⅠⅠ•———•ⅠⅠⅠ•———•ⅠⅠⅠ•❧

Τειρεσίας | Tye-ree-see-uhs / Tih-ray-see-uhs

T IRESIAS, THE BLIND PROPHET, is a recurring figure in Greek myth, making appearances in works by Sophocles, Euripides, and Ovid[1]. The son of a shepherd and a nymph, his life experiences are certainly interesting and unusual.

As a young man, Tiresias attracted Hera's rage, which would change his life. One day while walking in the mountains, he came across a pair of snakes mating in the middle of his path. Rather than leaving them alone, Tiresias lashed out at the snakes with his stick. When Hera heard what happened, her punishment was swift. Tiresias was transformed into a woman and made to work as a priestess of Hera. Tiresias remained a woman for seven years, even marrying and having children, until once again, she encountered the same snakes, on the same path and was returned to his male form.

According to ancient sources there are conflicting myths explaining the origin of Tiresias' blindness. In some accounts, his loss of sight is the price he pays for stumbling across Athena bathing. In others, Tiresias is called upon to settle an argument between Juno and Jupiter about which of the sexes derives the most "from the pleasures of love". Tiresias, having been both male and female, sides with Jupiter[2] much to Juno's chagrin, and is blinded for his trouble.

Tiresias' gift of prophecy, also bestowed by the gods, is presented as compensation for his blindness. In many of his appearances, Tiresias is sought out for his wisdom and foresight. Ironically, despite his literal blindness, Tiresias always sees the truth, his difficult and painful visions of the future foretelling the tragedy that follows, highlighting the metaphorical blindness of those in power.

In Homer's The Odyssey, Odysseus visits Hades to seek Tiresias' advice on how to get home – his wisdom is valued even after his death.

Suzanne Graham

58

Iphis (Ip)

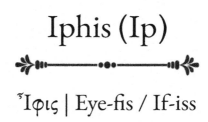

Ἶφις | Eye-fis / If-iss

IPHIS WAS BORN OF a humble father named Ligdus and a mother named Telethusa. Ligdus prayed to the gods that his wife would have an easy birth, and that she gave birth to a boy, as he was concerned with the trouble a girl would cause for them. He insisted that if the child was a girl, she should be killed. Telethusa pleaded for him to change his mind, but Ligdus would not yield.

Distraught, Telethusa had a vision of the goddess Isis among other Egyptian deities, who instructed her that she should keep her child and that her prayers would be answered should Telethusa need aid from the goddess.

Telethusa gave birth to a girl, and no one but she and the nurse knew of this, as Ligdus was not present. Telethusa rejoiced that Ligdus chose to name the child Iphis, a gender-neutral name. They raised Iphis as a son.

Ligdus found a bride for Iphis, Ianthe. The pair had been educated together, but Iphis was concerned about her feelings for Ianthe, as she felt they were unnatural. Telethusa delayed the wedding as long as possible, until both she and Iphis attended the temple of Isis to pray for her help. Telethusa threw herself across the altar and offered jewellery for the goddess, asking for assistance through tears.

The temple doors shook, light gleamed off of the image of the goddess, and the sistrum rattled after the prayer. As they left the temple, Iphis changed in physique and looks, and had become a man.

The story of Iphis has been explored in different aspects of the LGBTQ+ community, both as the only story of same-sex attraction between women in ancient Greek or Roman literature, and as a transgender narrative of Iphis's transition to marry Ianthe without further delay.

Aneirin Pendragon

90. *Iphis Isidis commiseratione ex puella in marem.*

59

Niobe (Nb)

Νιόβη | Ny-oh-bee / Nee-oh-bee

THE MORTAL NIOBE CAME from an infamous family, as she was the daughter of the damned Phrygian king Tantalus, sister of ill-fated Pelops, aunt of fratricidal Atreus. She had the honour of being betrothed to one of the Theban founders, Amphion. The marriage proved to be happy and fruitful, as they went on to have, in most accounts, seven sons and seven daughters.

Proud of both her children and her ability to beget such wonderful gifts, Niobe felt more and more comfortable boasting to anyone who would listen. At first, they were the effusive words of an overjoyed parent, however they soon began to tear down a fellow mother, Leto, whose children were no less than Apollo and Artemis. Why should people revere the mother of two gods that never even show themselves? Why not laud the woman who not only survived fourteen pregnancies but raised them all to be impressive, marriageable adults.

This pricked the ears of Apollo and Artemis, who would not stand for this slander of their mother nor the audacious example of hubris. They rained down slings of poison arrows, slaying all but one of the children in front of the devastated Niobe. She fled homeward to Mount Sipylus, collapsing into unceasing tears. She then underwent the classical trope of metamorphosis, becoming an unmoving yet ever weeping stone.

Romans and Greeks featured this story in art and literature, including being referenced in works such as the *Iliad* and *Antigone*, and later Renaissance painters also found this tale particularly evocative. Despite the ancient virtue of avoiding hubris, most references were to her lamentation and heartbreak. Even in modern society, we can commiserate with a mother who loved herself and her children so fiercely. Niobe shows us that we are all susceptible to putting family first to the point of detriment, despite the best intentions.

Katherine Livingston

Niobes liberi sagittis ab Apolline et Diana conficiuntur.

60

Pygmalion (Pg)

❧┉━━━━━●●●━━━━━┉❧

Πυγμαλίων | Pig-may-lee-on

K NOWN AS THE PROTAGONIST of the myth of 'Pygmalion and Galatea', Cypriot king and sculptor Pygmalion famously fell in love with one of his own creations.

Unimpressed by the women who surrounded him, Pygmalion swore off relationships for many years and instead embraced the art he so cherished; in his mind, women possessed so many unattractive qualities that it was not worth the trouble of sharing his life with one. Yet one fateful day, Pygmalion fashioned Galatea, an ivory maiden of such great beauty that even this snobbish artist developed an attraction to her. He began to court her, presenting this sculpture of his with lavish gifts and holding her as one would embrace a lover. Inanimate though she may have been, Pygmalion imagined Galatea to be a living being who returned his feelings and responded to his romantic gestures. Unfortunately, it would eventually dawn on him that his fantasies would remain exactly that, fantasies.

So it was that at the annual festival honouring the goddess Aphrodite, Pygmalion stood before her altar and prayed for the opportunity to marry his beloved Galatea – or at least a woman who might compare to her. Upon returning home, he was astonished to find that the gift of life had been bestowed upon his sculpture. Although he initially believed himself to be dreaming, Pygmalion was overcome with joy at the miraculous opportunity to wed the object of his affections.

This tale could be interpreted as a reflection on the fact that no individual can ever aspire to achieve perfection, or even find such a thing in others. Galatea is flawless in appearance, but her lack of substance does not satisfy Pygmalion's subconscious yearning for companionship. People and, by extension, connections, are far more interesting and impactful when they contain endearing qualities as well as imperfections.

The myth has gone on to inspire many works of art and fiction, such as George Bernard Shaw's 1913 play *Pygmalion,* which in turn would be adapted into the acclaimed 1956 musical *My Fair Lady*.

Carlotta Vincenzi

Dramatis Personae

I**T IS HARD TO** consider Greek myth without including some of the characters who we mostly know from Greek drama. The theatre, as we might recognise it today, evolved in ancient Greece in the sixth and fifth centuries BCE, and in that time, hundreds of plays – most of which are now lost to us – were written by the great playwrights of the time: Sophocles, Euripides, Aeschylus, Aristophanes, and others.

These plays give us some of the best-known characters from the Greek canon, whose stories tell us a great deal about the ancient world, as well as providing frameworks for discussions of our own time.

Antigone asks us, for example, if you had to choose between following the law, or following tradition, which would you choose? *Medea* asks us, what is the difference between justice and vengeance?

The blend of morality, philosophy, dialogue, and drama is irresistible.

Plays like Aeschylus's *Oresteia*, or Aristophanes's *The Frogs*, or Euripides's *Hippolytus* develop characters and plots found in Homer and other myths, so the sources entwine and enrich the mythology, casting new light and shadow on characters we might have believed we already knew.

And imagine compiling a volume such as this without including Oedipus, Lysistrata, Medea and the rest. Unthinkable!

Oedipus (Oe)

Οἰδίπους | Ed-ip-uss / Eed-ip-uss

OEDIPUS WAS THE KING of Thebes, a man who had everything: a stunning intellect, royal power, and a loving family, but he lost it all in a single day and became a symbol to the Greeks of the limits of human intelligence and the cruelty of inescapable fate...

Oedipus grew up in Corinth but left the city when the Oracle at Delphi prophesied that he would kill his father and sleep with his mother. He was determined not to see the prophecy fulfilled and so fled to Thebes. On his way there, he was assaulted on the road and killed his attacker in the fight. When he arrived at Thebes, he saved the people from the savage Sphinx by solving her devious riddle. The people were so grateful they made him king and he was married to Jocasta, the last king's widow.

Years later, a plague devastated Thebes, and the oracle advised it could be lifted by exiling the unknown murderer of Laius, the previous king. Oedipus sprang into action, but what he found would change his life forever. The traveller he had killed on the road was Laius, *he* was the murderer he was looking for and, worse still, Laius was his father, having abandoned him in the wilderness to be found by his Corinthian foster father. Most terrible of all, Jocasta was his mother! Overwhelmed by the horror of it all, Oedipus blinded himself and was exiled.

The story of Oedipus has fascinated people ever since, inspiring Sigmund Freud's idea of an 'Oedipus Complex'. More generally, the story of Oedipus forces us to confront our nature as humans, capable of extraordinary intelligence and extraordinary blindness, and question the nature of free will and the choices we make.

Derek McCann

63

Medea (Md)

⫸⫷

Μήδεια | Meh-dee-uh / Meh-day-uh

MAIDEN, MOTHER, MONSTER. PRINCESS, priestess, witch. Medea had as many faces as the goddess Hecate[1] whom she served. The Princess of Colchis was the granddaughter of the sun god Helios, his golden fire running through her veins as it did in her father's, the brutal King Aeëtes.

We first meet Medea in the epic tale of the Golden Fleece where the witch-maiden secures Jason's success in capturing the Golden Fleece from her father and escapes with him on the Argo. Whether Jason simply caught her eye or her fate was sealed by the gods in order to aid him, the stories vary.

During their escape we get the first hint of Medea's capability for horror, as the most blood-thirsty tellings have Medea chopping her brother into pieces and scattering them into the sea to stall their pursuers. On their arrival to Jason's homeland of Iolcus, she tricks King Pelias'[2] own daughters into slitting their father's throat. After this, Medea and Jason are exiled to Corinth where they have two children.

It is this part of the story that is most infamous – from Euripides and Seneca to the modern day. As Jason betrays Medea for a new Princess of Corinth, Medea submits to vengeance and fury. Sending a poisoned dress to the Princess, she is scorched to death alongside the King as he cradles her sizzling skin. Unsatisfied, Medea is driven to commit the most heinous crime: killing her own two children to spite Jason. In the unfolding chaos, she is aided by her grandfather Helios' chariot and flown away on dragon's wings to Athens where she marries King Aegeus, crossing paths with another hero, Theseus...

Another witch figure in Greek mythology, Circe, is Medea's aunt who aids her during her escape from King Aeëtes.

Jacqueline Munro

64

Electra (Ec)

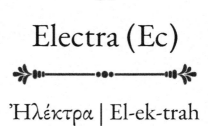

Ἠλέκτρα | El-ek-trah

Electra was the daughter of King Agamemnon and Queen Clytemnestra, and part of the cursed house of Atreus. To the ancient Greeks and Romans, Electra and her family acted as a sort of moral compass, revolving around the themes of Greek justice and revenge, as well as mourning in the ancient world.

Electra represents a tale of Greek justice: 'blood for blood' or 'an eye for an eye'. She plots with her brother, Orestes, to avenge the murder of Agamemnon by Clytemnestra, but in order to enact this revenge they have to kill their own mother. However, known sometimes only to the audience (and not Electra and Orestes), this murder of Agamemnon has been committed to avenge the murder of Electra's own sister (his daughter) Iphigenia, thus making the ancient Greeks question if their own system of revenge as a form of justice is wise. Or, as Sophocles sees it – leading to a cyclical violence that never ends.

Electra's intense grief at the loss of her father is representative of how Greek women are expected to act, both within the tradition of Greek tragedies and in ancient Greek society. However, Electra goes above and beyond this expected period of mourning for women, and still mourns her father 20 years after his death.

Although Electra's story and fate are often the result of those around her, Electra is one of the most popular tragic mythological characters. She is the main character in two Greek tragedies: *Electra* by Sophocles and *Electra* by Euripides. Alongside this, she is a central character in the *Oresteia Trilogy* by Aeschylus, *Orestes* by Euripides and her story has been revitalised in more modern adaptations, such as *Elektra* by Jennifer Saint in 2022.

Robyn Hayward

Non, fatal Etranger, je ne rendrai jamais

Ces préſens douloureux que ta pitié m'a faits ;

Oreste, act. 3. ſc. 4.

J. M. Moreau le J.e inv.   1783.   J. B. Simonet Sculp.

65

Creon (Cn)

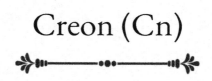

Κρέων | Cree-on / Cray-on

CREON WAS THE BROTHER of Jocasta, queen of Thebes. When Jocasta's husband was murdered and the Sphinx[1] took residence on the road to Thebes, Creon promised his sister's hand and the throne to whoever defeated the monster. Many tried and failed, but Oedipus eventually solved the riddle of the Sphinx,[2] and became king.

When a pestilence broke out, Creon was sent to interrogate the Oracle of Delphi[3] about it. After it was revealed that Oedipus was the reason for the plague as he had killed his own father and married his own mother, he left the city to his sons Eteocles and Polynices. The former refused to let his brother rule, so the other sieged Thebes with six allied armies.

Both brothers died during the war, so Creon became king, and ordered that Polynices should not be buried.[4] Antigone, Polynices' sister, disobeyed and was condemned to be buried alive for her crime. Her fiancé Haemon, son of Creon, decided to die with her, which caused Creon's wife to take her own life as well.

Creon kept ruling Thebes until his death. According to one tradition, he was killed in battle by the Athenian hero Theseus. In another, by the descendant of an earlier king of Thebes who then conquered the city.

Creon was a descendant of the Spartoi ('the sown ones'), warriors sprung out of the earth from the teeth of a dragon.

Kate Minniti

H6.

66

Lysistrata (Ly)

❧⊱━━━━━•••━━━━━⊰❧

Λυσιστράτη | Ly-sist-rata / Lye-sis-trah-ta

MOST COMMONLY KNOWN AS the woman who organised a sex strike to end a war, Lysistrata is the titular character of the comedy by the same name by ancient Greek playwright Aristophanes. The play was first shown in 411 BCE amid the rumblings of another conflict between Athens and Sparta.

Lysistrata, whose name means "disbander of armies" in ancient Greek, leads the women from both sides of the Peloponnesian War. Appealing to the women's love of their husbands (and lovers), Lysistrata faces difficulty in unifying the women, as they are filled with as much desire as the men. Ultimately she succeeds in making them all swear an in-depth oath abstaining from sex.

With the help of Aphrodite, the younger women begin their strike, refusing to do any domestic work, including sexual acts. The older women are aided by Athena to occupy the Acropolis to prevent the funds there being used for the dispute. She is even successful in chasing away the magistrate and the police with the help of the women coming together against their foe.

Soon enough, in less than a week, the men cave, overcome by their desires. They ask Lysistrata to aid in the peace negotiations, thereby ending both the strike and the war. The play ends with everyone celebrating Athena, finally united under one banner.

Many modern scholars consider the comedy to be feminist and anti-war, as the main plot shows a woman taking a stand against more lives lost. Others argue that the play was intended to be neither of these things, as there are sexist remarks throughout and no clear stance regarding war in the real world, especially as peace is established as a way of ending the strike rather than the hostility.

Ellana Thornton-Wheybrew

LYSISTRATA.

67

Prometheus (Pm)

Προμηθεύς | Pruh-mee-thee-us

A MEMBER OF THE generation before the Olympian gods, Prometheus sided with the newcomers against most of the Titans. He is best remembered for two stories about tricks he played, which put him in parallel with other cultural fire-givers and trickster archetypes (Loki, Lucifer, Coyote, etc). These tricks were for the benefit of humanity but angered the gods, leading to his punishment.

The first story involves meeting with Zeus to decide how much of their food humans ought to sacrifice to the gods, and how much they will be allowed to keep for themselves to live on. Prometheus dresses up the two portions deceptively and Zeus picks the one that turns out to be just bones and fat, leaving the edible meat for the people. In Hesiod's telling, Zeus actually sees through the trick but picks wrongly anyway just so he has an excuse to punish Prometheus.

In the second story, Prometheus gives humanity fire, smuggling it out of Olympus in a fennel stalk. Depending on the storyteller, Prometheus stole fire (symbolising intelligence or creativity) either to make up for other animals' biological advantages – claws, spines, venom – or because Zeus had previously taken fire away. The story of Pandora is also connected to Prometheus and punishing humanity.

Prometheus's ultimate punishment was to be chained to a mountain in the Caucasus, where every day an eagle pecked out his liver, and every night it grew back. Eventually, Heracles freed him.

Today Prometheus has become a symbol of enlightenment and innovation, but also a warning against pride and 'playing God.' Mary Shelley subtitled her novel *Frankenstein* 'The Modern Prometheus.' J. Robert Oppenheimer, who developed the first atomic weapons at Los Alamos in 1945, was called 'The American Prometheus' for the fearsome firepower he and his colleagues gave to mankind.

The name 'Prometheus' might mean 'thinking ahead' or 'thief'!

Daniel Galef

68

Cassandra (Ca)

――――――◆‖‖――――●●●――――‖‖◆――――

Κασσάνδρα | Cah-sand-rah

CASSANDRA WAS A TROJAN Princess, daughter of the King and Queen Priam and Hecuba.

She was a prophetess, and there are a few versions of how she gained this power. One version says that she and her twin brother Helenus were left overnight in the temple of Apollo and had their ears licked by snakes. Another, more well-known version, tells the story that Apollo desired her. Cassandra agreed to sleep with Apollo in return for the gift of prophecy. Cassandra then refused to lie with Apollo, and in his anger, he cursed her to never be believed, as he was not able to take away her gift.

Cassandra foresaw many things that were not believed. She predicted that Paris and Helen's elopement would end in the fall of Troy, and yet Paris still went. She predicted that the wooden horse was full of Greek soldiers and tried to destroy it, but was held back by the Trojans.

During the fall of Troy, Cassandra hid in the temple of Athena. Despite clinging to the statue of Athena, Ajax the Lesser dragged her from the temple and raped her. Athena, offended by this, caused the death of Ajax as he returned home.

Cassandra also predicted her own murder, along with the murder of Agamemnon at the hands of his wife and her lover. Agamemnon had taken Cassandra captive after defeating the Trojans, and on their arrival in Mycenae, both were killed, either by Clytemnestra herself, or by her lover Aegisthus, depending on the version of the story you read.

It is suggested by Pausanias that there was a temple built to honour Cassandra in Sparta, where she was also known as Alexandra.

Even now, her name is used to describe someone who successfully predicts disaster but is not believed.

Zoe Lister

69

Antigone (Ag)

━━━━━━━━━━━━━━━━

Ἀντιγόνη | Ann-tig-oh-nee

ANTIGONE, MYTHOLOGICAL PRINCESS OF Thebes, was one of four children born to the incestuous marriage of Oedipus and his mother Jocasta. After Oedipus uncovers the truth of his incest and blinds himself in shame, Antigone followed him into self-imposed exile. She led him to Colonus, where Theseus, king of Athens, offered sympathy and Athenian citizenship to Oedipus.

In Oedipus's absence, his sons Eteocles and Polynices agreed to share power, alternating their rule of Thebes each year. When Eteocles reneged and refused to hand power over, Polynices gathered an army and prepared to attack the city.

Oedipus died in Colonus, and Antigone returned to Thebes with her sister Ismene. She couldn't prevent Polynices from attacking; he and Eteocles killed each other and power passed to their uncle Creon. Creon branded Polynices a traitor for attacking his own city. He forbade anyone from burying or mourning Polynices, upon pain of death. Without proper burial rites, Polynices' soul would not find peace in the Underworld.

Antigone fiercely defended her brother's right to a burial and was willing to die to uphold what she believed was divine justice. Despite Ismene's pleas for her to not bring further misery to their family, Antigone defied Creon's orders and buried Polynices.

She remained defiant even after she had been caught. Creon, furious at her disobedience and resistance to his rule, ordered her to be entombed in a cave and buried alive. Although he was eventually convinced of his own injustice, he was too late to save her: Antigone had already hanged herself.

Antigone's youthful idealism and unwavering defiance against injustice has seen her story retold throughout the generations. Jean Anouil draws parallels between Antigone and the French Resistance in her play *Antigone*, and Kamila Shamsie's Antigone fights for the repatriation of her brother's body after he is killed escaping ISIS in *Home Fire*.

Natasha Hershaw

70

Agamemnon (Am)

━━━━━━━━━━━━━━

Ἀγαμέμνων | A-ga-mem-non

AGAMEMNON, KING OF MYCENAE, was the son of Atreus and the most powerful king in Greece. Agamemnon and his younger brother Menelaus, king of Sparta, married the daughters of Tyndareus and Leda, Clytemnestra and Helen respectively. Agamemnon and Clytemnestra had one son, Orestes, and two daughters, Electra and Iphigenia.

After Helen was 'stolen' by the Trojan prince Paris and taken to Troy, Agamemnon led a Greek expedition against the Trojans to avenge the insult. The Greek forces mustered at the natural harbour of Aulis in ancient Boeotia, but unfavourable winds sent by the goddess Artemis prevented the Greek troops from sailing. There are several versions of the story as to why Artemis sent the winds, but one thing they all agree on is that Agamemnon caused her offence. In order to calm the contrary winds and appease Artemis' anger, the religious seer[1] Calchas tells Agamemnon that he is required to sacrifice his daughter, Iphigenia, if he is to sail to Troy. On the pretext of being married to the great hero Achilles, Iphigenia comes to Aulis and is sacrificed by her father (a real red wedding!).

Homer's *Iliad* centres around Achilles and his quarrel with Agamemnon. In Book One of the *Odyssey*, Homer briefly mentions that on his return home Agamemnon is murdered in revenge by his wife Clytemnestra and her lover (Agamemnon's cousin) Aegisthus. Agamemnon's return home and murder was a popular myth used by later authors, most famously the Athenian playwright Aeschylus.

It is debatable whether Agamemnon was real or not. In 1876 German archaeologist Heinrich Schliemann discovered a gold funerary mask at Mycenae, which he believed to be the mask of Agamemnon – though its authenticity has been roundly questioned.

Agamemnon's father Atreus killed his brother Thyestes' children and fed them to him, which Thyestes ate unknowingly.

Dr. Simon Trafford

71

Clytemnestra (Ct)

————————————

Κλυταιμνήστρα | Kly-tem-neh-struh / Kly-tuhm-nee-struh

IN GREEK MYTHOLOGY, CLYTEMNESTRA was the wife of Agamemnon, and the sister of Helen of Troy. She is most famous for killing her husband, upon his return from Troy, by trapping him in a net while he took a bath.

She was a woman scorned, murdering Agamemnon to avenge the death of her daughter Iphigenia, whom Agamemnon "sacrificed" at Aulis, after the seer Calchas prophesied that the lack of wind, in their bid to sail to Troy, would be remedied with the sacrificial killing. She also had an affair with her husband's cousin Aegisthus, whose father and brothers were murdered by Atreus, Agamemnon's father. In a later version, she had a previous husband, Tantalus, whom Agamemnon slaughtered, along with her infant son.

The murder of Agamemnon takes place in the first of a trilogy of tragedies by the playwright Aeschylus, called the *Oresteia*,[1] and in the second play Clytemnestra is murdered (along with Aegisthus) by her son Orestes, avenging the death of his father.

Clytemnestra is an important female character in mythology. She is one of only a few women who are represented as having strength and autonomy, and her actions are often likened to those of men. In the ancient world, that was a significant, and worrisome, comparison because women were thought to be irrational and impulsive. In Aeschylus' tragedies in particular, this theme mirrored anxieties about the politics of the time, in particular the fear of anti-democratic challengers.

Later receptions conceptualise the character with a feminist viewpoint (much like Medea) refocusing Clytemnestra's story, and centralising her role as a mother and a fighter, whose revenge on her husband is the culmination of years of abuse; the breaking point is the death of her daughter.

Georgina Homer

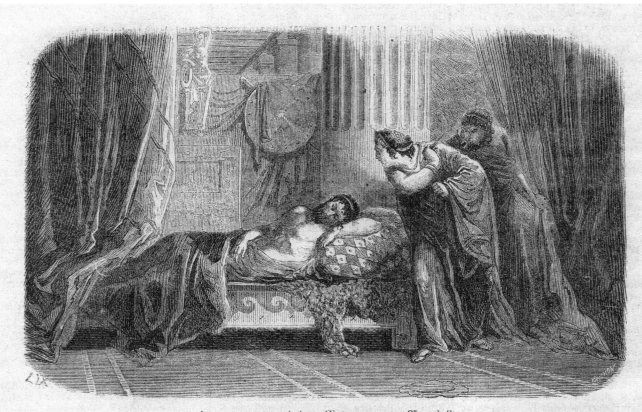

Agamemnon assassiné par Clytemnestre (p. 35, col. 3).

72

Andromache (Ad)

❦┅┅——•••——┅┅❦

Ἀνδρομάχη | Ann-drom-a-key

ANDROMACHE WAS ONE OF four significant females from Homer's *Iliad*. She was Trojan Hector's noble wife, and Astyanax's mother. Her father, King Eetion of Cilician Thebe, and seven brothers, were murdered by Achilles. Her mother, enslaved by Achilles, was sold back for a high ransom, and shot dead by Artemis. Hector and Astyanax were her only surviving family.

Hector was Andromache's world. Ancient Greek society was rooted in gender rules and patriarchy[1] so without him, Andromache's life was meaningless. Unfortunately, Hector was fighting a war caused by his brother, Paris, stealing Menelaus' Spartan wife, Helen. The gods were involved and taking sides. If Hector died, Andromache would become a war prize. Despite Andromache's pleas not to widow her, Hector's public duty took priority over his familial one. War was the task of men. Cowardice was unthinkable. Upon returning to the fight, Achilles killed Hector, cementing Andromache's future and Astyanax's death.

Euripides continued Andromache's story in *Andromache* as the war prize of Neoptolemus, Achilles' son. Hermione, Helen's daughter, now Neoptolemus' wife, felt threatened by Andromache, and schemed against her. Despite her name's meaning ('fighter of men'), and being a foreign-born barbarian, Andromache was no warrior. Her traits as the ideal wife and mother helped her survive. As a slave and concubine, Andromache remained noble, more so than either Helen or Hermione. Euripides ended her story by having Peleus and Thetis, Achilles' parents, rescue her. Andromache would marry Hector's brother, Helenus, raise a new line of kings, and Troy would live again.

Through *The Iliad* to *Andromache*, deaths and war impacted heavily on Andromache. Repeatedly exposed to trauma, unable to process one before being subjected to another, Andromache was expected to accept her fate without question. Fast-forward to modernity, it seems nothing has changed. Women and children suffer while the menfolk fight.

Amanda D Binns

73

Dionysus (Dy)

⊰⊱———••————⊰⊱

Διόνυσος | Die-oh-ny-sus / Die-oh-nee-sus

D IONYSUS WAS THE SON of Zeus and Semele, a mortal daughter of Cadmus the king of Thebes. Out of jealousy, Hera, Zeus's godly wife, persuaded the pregnant Semele that she should make sure that Zeus really was as divine as he claimed to be. When Semele asked Zeus to show her his true form, he did, but this was too much for a mortal and she was blasted by thunderbolts. Zeus saved the fetal Dionysus by sewing him into his thigh and keeping him there until he was ready to be born. When Dionysus was born, Zeus gave him to Hermes who in turn took him to be raised by the maenads or nymphs of Nysa – a distant, eastern country.

When Dionysus was older, his nymph nurses accompanied him back to Thebes as the Bacchae. Upon arrival, he demanded to be recognized as a god. From there grew many stories of him demanding his recognition with fatal, often transformative consequences.[1]

To the ancient Greeks, Dionysus was the breaker of social boundaries. Depicted in various forms – as a man or a beast with a beard, as a youth, or holding a thyrsus[2] while donning an ivy wreath and wearing a gender-ambivalent chiton[3] – he represented the liminal spaces in society. The ancient Greeks felt his presence by drinking wine, wearing masks in the theatre, and through entering into ritualistic frenzy.[4] Often, this would be thought of as Dionysus possessing the person performing these acts.

Our love for Dionysus has not waned. We see him in music like *Dionysus* by BTS and *The Cult of Dionysus* by the Orion Experience, cartoons like Disney's "Pastoral Symphony" in *Fantasia*, and in books like *The Secret History* by Donna Tartt and the *Percy Jackson* Series as Mr. D, the abrasive yet lovable camp director.

Talia BarNoy

BACCHI et ARIADNÆ.
Felix Congressus.

Desertæ et multa querenti   Amplexusque et opem Liber tulit.

Ant. Coypel Pinx.

ord. B. Picart.

74

Iphigenia (Ih)

Ἰφιγένεια | If-ih-jen-yuh / If-uh-jen-ee-ah

IPHIGENIA WAS A TRAGIC heroine who was the subject of two Greek plays by Euripides. Although she does not appear in the *Iliad*, Iphigenia was known to the ancient Greeks as an integral part of the beginning of the Trojan War.

Iphigenia was the daughter of king Agamemnon and queen Clytemnestra. During a hunt, while the war party bound for Troy were assembled at Aulis,[1] Agamemnon killed a deer in a grove sacred to Artemis. In revenge, the goddess caused the winds to die down, beaching the ships. Agamemnon turned to the seer Calchas to find a solution. Calchas told him of Artemis' anger, and that in recompense, she would only accept the sacrifice of his daughter Iphigenia.

Believing himself to have no other option, Agamemnon sent for Iphigenia by pretending that she was going to marry the hero Achilles. When Iphigenia and her mother Clytemnestra arrived at Aulis, they discovered that the wedding was a lie. Although Achilles, who was not involved in the conspiracy, promised to try and save her life, Iphigenia willingly faced her fate. Some versions of the myth say that at the last minute, Artemis snatched the girl up and replaced her with a deer. Iphigenia then became a priestess of Artemis.

Iphigenia's fate is not very well explored in modern texts, but she is the protagonist of Euripides' *Iphigenia in Aulis*, which describes Agamemnon's plot to sacrifice his daughter, and the play *Iphigenia Among the Taurians* by the same playwright, in which Iphigenia is a priestess of Artemis in Crimea.

Aimee Hinds Scott

75

Xerxes (X)

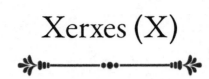

Ξέρξης | Zerk-sees / Zerk-zees

Xerxes was the Great King of Persia, the ruler of all Asia. He invaded the independent city-states of mainland Greece with a vast army in 380 / 379 BCE, as his own father, Darius, had attempted unsuccessfully in the past.

That the small Greek city-states repelled the Persian army was a matter of intense and enduring pride to all Greeks. This achievement was seen as tantamount to those of the Trojan War itself. Through it, the Greeks ensured their continuing freedom and independence – for a time, at least!

The achievements of the Greeks against the Persians were soon recounted, immortalised, embellished, and fictionalised in various ways, including in Greek drama. The play, *The Persians*, by the tragedian Aeschylus, was first performed in 472 BCE in Athens and centres upon Xerxes. Events are presented from the Persian perspective, as news reaches the royal household in Susa (capital of the Persian Achaemenid Empire), of their catastrophic defeat, with deaths beyond counting.

This is all portrayed as the sole fault of ill-considered decisions by the young and impetuous King Xerxes. An unending series of disasters is recounted, suggested through dreams, and prophesied. Through this, famous Greek victories against Persia are referenced from the past (Marathon), present (Salamis), and future (Plataea). When Xerxes himself finally enters in tattered clothes, all he can now command is lamentation, for the Greek gods punish those who overreach themselves.

Herodotus' *Histories* gives a different account of Xerxes. The Persian wars established factors that would ultimately lead to the campaigns of Alexander the Great (of neighbouring Macedon) and establish his empire.

The modern graphic novel *Xerxes* tells a version of events from Marathon right through to the death of Alexander. The very stylised films *300*, and *300: Rise of an Empire* are partly based on this comic series.

Isabel Hood

Primordial Gods

PRIMORDIAL MEANS, LITERALLY, THE first order, or the first generation. The first group of gods in existence, according to Greek mythology, were representations of forces, powers and occasionally abstract ideas, all of which were fundamental to human life.

As their name suggests, they were the first entities in all creation. Out of Chaos (disorder) came the Cosmos (order). If you like, they were the first things the Greeks believed had been created by the Big Bang: fundamental things like the earth, the mountains, the sea, the sky, the air, darkness, the day, the night, power, desire and the underworld.

Sometimes these originating deities can be seen in opposing pairs, such Nyx (Night) being the mother of Hemera (Day), and Erebus (Darkness) the father of the bright sky (Aether), and so on.

While these deities have fewer myths written about them than the later Titans and Olympians, these gods feature in the background of almost all of them, and their place in the genealogy of myth marks them as the originators from whom all other myths had to spill...

Chaos (Xx)

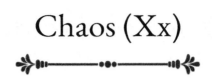

Χάος | Kay-oss / Kah-oss

"IN THE VERY BEGINNING, Chaos came to be." In Hesiod's poem *Theogony* (literally, *How Gods Came to Be*), Chaos comes first. Out of Chaos the first generation of primordial deities – Gaea, Tartarus, Eros, Erebus, and Nyx – are born. These children of Chaos we call *binatural* gods: Gaea, for example, is *both* the physical Earth and humanoid Earth goddess. But what of Chaos *itself*? Or should we say *themself*? Chaos is a 'neuter noun' – neither masculine nor feminine – the only *agender* god in the Hellenic pantheon, if even a god at all.

Chaos is closely related to the word *chasm*, derived from the Greek χάσκω, meaning *yawn* or *gape*. It is a *gap*, a void, a negative space defined not by tangible matter, but its absence. Greek philosophers have interpreted it accordingly: the airy realm above or below the earth, the empty space where atoms whirl, or the receptacle of form and substance from the higher, ideal world. Theologians had other ideas: it is the *abyss*, the primordial waters from which everything arose, either spontaneously or when the *breath of god came upon* it.

The chronological *chasm* between Hesiod's Greece and Ovid's Rome teemed with these ideas, which influenced the latter in his *Metamorphoses*: Chaos was not a whole lot of nothing, but of *everything*, a giant blob of undifferentiated stuff. This unity was not harmonious, but a *conflict* of elements in a *legal* sense (the Latin is *līs*, root of *litigation*), requiring the intervention of a "god and better nature" to do it *justice* by *separating* everything out, sorted into its proper place.

Today, the law of *entropy* suggests everything is subject to ultimately decaying: order must return to disorder, to constituent elements, to nothingness. Perhaps the ancients were on to something about Chaos being the principle of our existence.

Dr. Jeremy Swist

OVIDII METAM. LIB. I.
Aº 1589
1
E tenebris, deforme Chaos secessit oborta
Luce, suoq; loco sunt queq; Elementa locata
Astra polo radiant, quibus imminet igneus Æther,
Aera subsequitur Pontus, subit vltima Tellus.

78

Ouranos (Ou)

━━━━━◦•◦━━━━━

Οὐρανός | Yoo-ran-oss / You-ray-nus

OURANOS, ALSO KNOWN AS Uranus or Caelus in Roman mythology, is a celestial entity of great significance in Greek mythology. He is considered one of the primordial deities, born from Chaos, the formless void that existed before the creation of the world. Ouranos is often associated with the sky, and his name is indicative of his role as the personification of the heavens.

In Greek mythology, Ouranos is typically depicted as a vast, starry expanse that arches over the Earth. He is married to Gaia, the Earth itself, and together they are the parents of the Titans, the Cyclopes, and the Hecatonchires[1]. Ouranos' actions and relationships play a pivotal role in several key mythological narratives.

One of the most well-known stories involving Ouranos is his conflict with his own offspring. He feared the power of the Titans, his children, and in his attempts to maintain control, he imprisoned them deep within the Earth. This led to the rebellion of his son Cronus, who eventually overthrew Ouranos with the help of his mother Gaia. This story highlights the themes of generational conflict and the inevitability of change, which are common in Greek mythology.

Ouranos' significance extends beyond his role in this particular myth. As the personification of the sky, he embodies the infinite expanse above the Earth. This celestial realm was a source of wonder and inspiration for the ancient Greeks, and it played a crucial role in their understanding of the cosmos.

Ouranos' stories, especially the conflict with his children, are emblematic of the broader themes that run through Greek mythology, offering insights into the ancient Greek worldview and their understanding of the natural and supernatural realms. Ouranos, the celestial deity, remains a powerful symbol of the boundless and mysterious nature of the heavens.

Francesco Paolo Dal Rio

79

Erebus (Eb)

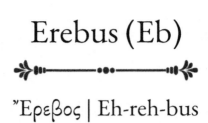

Ἔρεβος | Eh-reh-bus

T O THE ANCIENT GREEKS, Erebus represented darkness, a primordial deity present at the very beginning of the world in the myth of creation. In this role, Erebus later came to represent death and became poetically synonymous with the Underworld (also referred to as Tartarus or Hades). Unlike the humanoid Olympian gods, Erebus was a personified force described as a formless, abstract void of darkness.

There is more than one version of the ancient Greek creation myth. In one, at the very beginning of the world, there was first Chaos, a formless abyss from whom both Nyx (Night) and Erebus were born. These two primordial deities in turn gave birth to Aether (Bright Air) and Hemera (Day). In another version, Nyx lays an egg in the infinite depths of Erebus from which Eros (Love) is born.

In mythology, Erebus, sometimes described as one of the two divisions of the Underworld alongside Tartarus, was the location of famous mythological creatures such as Cerberus – the three-headed dog – and the Furies. It was further believed that souls passed through Erebus immediately after death, seen in Homer's *Iliad* and *Odyssey*, where Erebus represents the liminal space joining the living world to that of the Underworld.

The Romans recognized Erebus and Nyx as a pair and labelled them the parents of a whole host of dreadful forces such as Toil, Envy, and Old Age. In later Latin literature, Proserpina (Persephone) was called the "Queen of Erebus," a title indicative of her status as an underworld deity. In the modern world, Erebus lends his name to a strange host of things: the *Erebidae* family of moths, a ship lost in the Canadian Arctic in the 1800's only to have been recently recovered, and a *Warhammer* Dark Apostle and devout servant to Chaos.

Amanda Rivera

1.   *Orbis fabrica.*

80

Hemera (Hm)

❧━━━●┅●━━━❧

Ἡμέρα | He-mare-a / Hem-eh-ra

To the ancient Greeks, Hemera was the personification[1] of the day.

Hemera was the daughter of Erebus (Darkness) and Nyx (Night), and sister to Aether (Bright Sky). She was usually identified in the context of other gods, and was closely associated with Eos (Dawn), and Hera (queen of the Olympian gods, and goddess of the sky).

Hemera's role was to dispel the night and reveal the day. In the evening Hemera's mother, Nyx, would draw a dark veil across the sky, bringing night to the earth by blocking out the light of Aether. In the morning Hemera would disperse the mists of Nyx, allowing the light of Aether to shine back down on the earth. According to Hesiod, Nyx and Hemera passed by each other, but never dwelt in the same space at the same time: one was always passing over the earth, while the other waited for their turn.

Over time, Hemera and Eos became interchangeable, until Hemera was completely subsumed by Eos and disappeared as a separate deity altogether. The mythology surrounding Hemera is sparse, often focusing on Eos instead, and there is little indication that Hemera ever received a cult following of her own.

Hemera's Roman counterpart was Dies (Day), but she had a different genealogy to Hemera and a separate mythology.

Chrissie Downton

81

Ophion (Op)

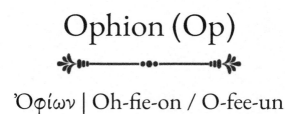

Ὀφίων | Oh-fie-on / O-fee-un

"SNAKES... WHY DID IT have to be snakes?" Indiana Jones' fear is an ancient fear, and Greek mythology has no shortage of frightening serpents, from Medusa's mane to terrifying Typhon. One of the most enigmatic is Ophion, a monster from the idiosyncratic mythology of the philosopher Pherecydes of Syros. Reputed to have taught Pythagoras and learned Phoenician wisdom, Pherecydes was praised by Aristotle for mixing myth with reason.

In Pherecydes' telling, the universe springs from the eternal triad, Zas, Chronos, and Chthonie, akin to Hesiod's Zeus, Cronos, and Gaia. Like the Egyptian creator-god Atum-Rē, Chronos' spilled seed generates the world, but eventually, paralleling Typhon and Echidna, the gods are opposed by monstrous (but undescribed) Ophion, who comes to rule Olympus with his mate Eurynome and their offspring, the Ophionidae. However, Cronos and Rhea cast them down into the depths of Ōgenos (the ocean). As Ophion is likely the offspring of Zas and Chthonie, this conflict serves as another episode of generational revolt like Ouranus against Cronos or Cronos against Zeus. Though we know nothing more of Ophion, his serpentine name containing ὄφις (ophis) "snake" may be a clue to his origin.

From Babylonia's Marduk vs Tiamat to Job's Yahweh vs Leviathan, from the Hittites' Tarḫunz vs Illuyanka to the Vedas' Indra vs. Vrtra to Zeus vs. Typhon, sky-gods routinely slay giant serpents in cultures around the world, a mythic archetype called a Chaoskampf. Calvert Watkins' How to Kill a Dragon describes an ancient poetic formula for dragonslaying found across Indo-European languages from Irish to Sanskrit, reconstructed as *g^{wh}ént $h_1$óg^{wh}im "he slew the serpent". The Greek descendant of *$h_1$óg^{wh}im is Ophion, making him the unique being in the Greek tradition who both plays a role in a Chaoskampf and whose name etymologically relates to this ancient trope. Thus Ophion affords us a glimpse of an alternative, non-Hesiodic theogony[1] connected to ophidian[2] archetypes from Greece's deepest Indo-European and Mediterranean roots.

Doug Henning

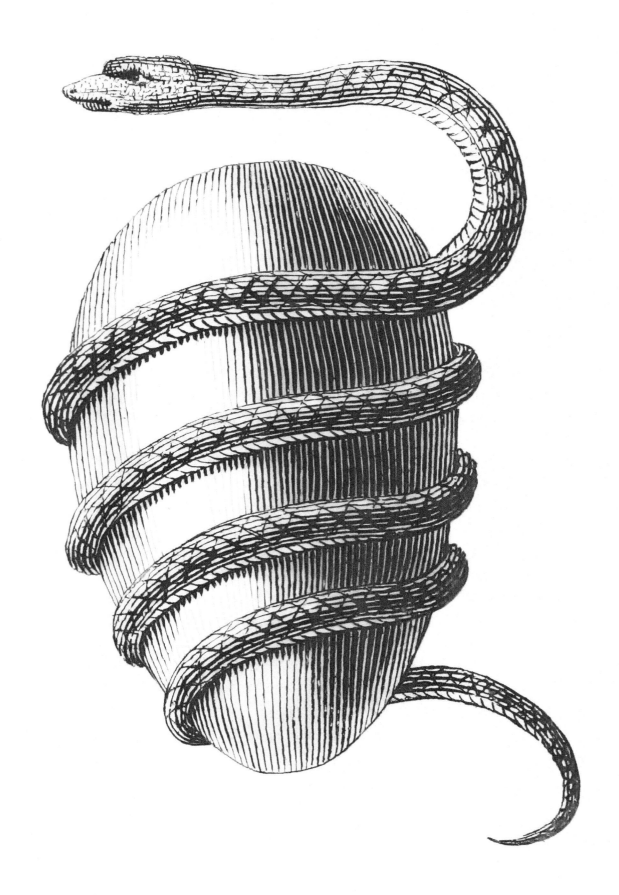

82

Aion (Ao)

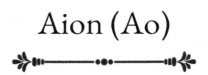

Αἰών | Eye-ohn / Eye-on / Ay-on

AION WAS A HELLENISTIC god associated with time, the zodiac, and the circle (or orb) which surrounded the universe. Aion was the god of perpetual or everlasting time, eternity – not to be confused with Cronos who was the god of empirical time, divided into past, present, and future. Aion's "time" was unbounded, cyclic: the future is a returning version of the past (this was later called "Aevum"). In depictions, he is usually semi-naked and surrounded by a large circle representing the zodiac and everlasting time.

There are few stories about Aion that we know of today, but through being combined with other major mythological figures, he managed to stay relevant even during Roman times. He combined with major figures such as Ouranos -- primordial god of the sky -- and Cronos – the Titan.

Mainly, though, he was affiliated with the mystery religions[1] associated with the afterlife in the later Classical era. These included the Dionysian mysteries, Orphic religion, and Mithraic mysteries. In these mystery religions, he was combined with Dionysus and Mithras, respectively. In the Imperial era, Aion (and his female counterpart "Aeternitas") both became symbols of rebirth and were associated with the Phoenix on coins produced by Antoninus Pius.

Aion, alone, however, became a symbol and a patron of the perpetuity of the Roman Empire. He is typically accompanied by a mother or Earth goddess such as Cybele or Tellus.

Aion as a deity is not remembered in the modern world, but the concept of perpetual, eternal time that he represented plays a very prevalent role in modern culture: from books, comics, and tv shows to science, religion, and philosophy. For many people, the concept of eternity changed the very way they lived. Aion is not only relevant to the modern world, for many people, especially those of a spiritual viewpoint, he is a fundamental part of it.

Ciaran Tolland

83

Nesoi (Ns)

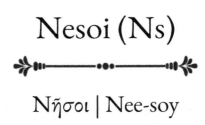

Νῆσοι | Nee-soy

THE NESOI WERE PRIMORDIAL goddesses that personified islands, with each island having its own personification and personality.

Primordial deities were the first generation of gods and goddesses, representing physical places and abstract concepts. Primordial deities included Gaia (Earth), Tartarus (Underworld), and Ouranus (Sky). While the later gods – Titans and Olympians – were given physical forms and patronage of things, the primordial deities were not embodied in the same way.

The Nesoi are referred to in Callimachus' *Hymn 4 to Delos*, where islands including Delos, Phoenician Cyrnus, Macris, and Cyprus are personified, and described as following in one another's footsteps. For Callimachus, the Nesoi come from a fight between Poseidon and Ourea (Mountains), during which Poseidon smote the mountains and cast the islands into the sea. From there, he rooted the islands' foundations into the seabed, so that they might forget the mainland.

The Nesoi also feature in the myth of Apollo and Artemis' birth. Leto, pregnant with the twins, is forced to wander the earth by the jealous Hera. Labouring, she comes to the Nesoi of the sea, but they all rebuke her on the orders of Iris (the messenger goddess of rainbows). To avoid Leto, the Nesoi 'fled all together, every one that she came to, along the waters'. Leto goes to the isle of Kos, but Apollo – from the womb – begs her not to birth him there.

The Nesoi have fallen into obscurity in the modern world. This is unsurprising, since they were not actively worshipped in the ancient world, nor did they take an active role in any myths. Although it would be interesting to read a myth from the perspective of the island it was happening on!

Dr. Shelby Judge

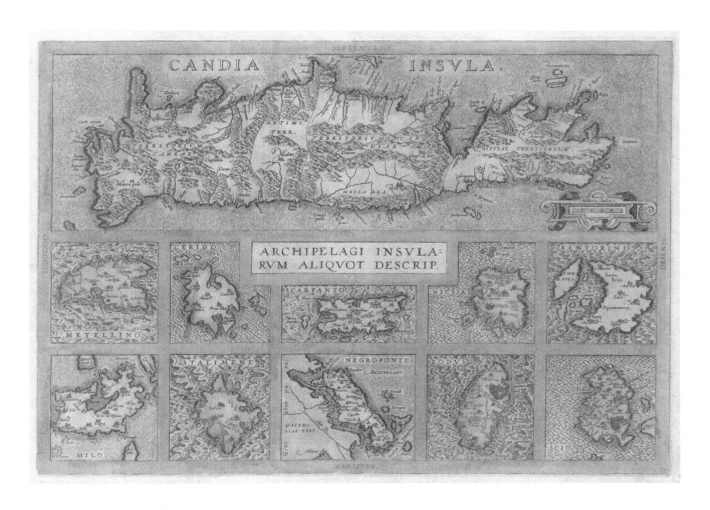

84

Gaia (G)

Γαῖα | Guy-ah / Gay-ah

GAIA IS THE MOTHER of all, one of the first primordial deities through whom all else came to be. Her name is the ancient Greek word for 'Earth', and she is synonymous with the land itself. The ancient Greeks respected and worshipped her because of this, viewing her as the bringer and taker of life. She was worshipped often as part of Demeter's cults, but also independently across the ancient Greek world.

As she was one of the first beings to exist, she created several deities without a partner, amongst whom was Ouranos (Sky). With Ouranos, she bore the Titans, the Cyclopes and Hecatonchires, but the latter two filled their father with such hatred of their monstrosity that he hid them away inside the earth as soon as they were born,[1] and continued to lay with Gaia. Eventually the pain and suffering of this got too much, and Gaia convinced the youngest Titan, Cronos, to castrate his father, which ended Ouranos' lusty behaviour.

Elsewhere, Gaia appeared at key moments: telling Cronos he would be overthrown by his son; advising Rhea on how to save Zeus from being eaten; prophesying that Zeus would win the battle against the Titans if he freed the Cyclopes and Hecatonchires. However, she did not always simply provide advice. When Zeus imprisoned the Titans, she called her children, the Giants, into battle with the Olympians; and when the Olympians won, she bore a fearsome monster named Typhon to attack Zeus.

Gaia is still worshipped in the modern day in a lot of pagan and Wiccan practices, who honour her as Mother Earth.

Gaia also raised Erichthonius, who would go on to become king of Athens, and set up the first worship of the goddess Athena there.

Midah Guilbaud-Walter

85

Pontus (Pu)

⋇⟊⟊⟊━━━━⟊•⟊━━━━⟊⟊⟊⋇

Πόντος | Pon-tus

FOR THE ANCIENT GREEKS, Pontus was the primordial god of the sea, and the embodiment of the sea itself. Pontus was a protogenoi[1], one of the ancient elemental beings that existed when the Earth was without shape or form. The Greeks and Romans would frequently personify the powerful elemental forces of the natural world, and worship them as deities. In mythology, stories that help explain the creation or properties of an aspect of the world are known as "etiological tales".

In surviving ancient literature, Pontus is not assigned human traits or personality like later Greek gods. He was a son of Gaia, and it was said by the ancient Greek poet Hesiod that he was born of no father; while later Roman author Hyginus describes him as the result of a union between Aether and Gaia. Pontus bore a number of children with his mother; including Nereus, Phorcys, Thaumas, Ceto, and Eurybia. Nereus was said to be gentle and true, and came to be known along with his brother Phorcys as; "The Old Man of the Sea". With Thalassa, Pontus is said to be the father of all oceanic life, as well as the Telchines[2].

It is hard to say for sure how Pontus was seen by the Greeks. In surviving Greco-Roman mosaics, he is often depicted as heavily muscled, with long hair, a wavy beard, and two crab leg horns rising from his head. Pontus is very seldom depicted in literature and art, apart from his birth, his consorts, and their resulting children. Later gods of the sea such as the Titan Oceanus and the Olympian Poseidon are far more present in art and literature. *Póntos* seems to have faded into obscurity, but his name lived on in ancient Greek as a common noun meaning "sea".

Douglas Jones

86

Nyx (Nx)

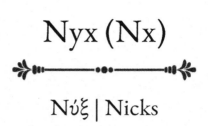

Νύξ | Nicks

NYX, THE GODDESS AND personification of the night, stands at the very beginning of the Greek creation story as told by Hesiod. Born out of the primordial Chaos, Nyx coupled with her brother Erebus (Darkness) and bore two children very unlike their parents: Aether (Bright Sky) and Hemera (Day). The Greeks saw the cycle of day and night as an endless heavenly charioteer race and often portrayed it on their pottery: Nyx, a winged figure, would ride the skies along other celestial deities, such as Selene (Moon), Helios (Sun) and Eos (Dawn). After her ride, Nyx returned to her underworld house, which she shared with Hemera. The mother and the daughter could never meet inside, though: as one would enter, another would leave.

After bringing forth Aether and Hemera, Hesiod narrates, Nyx procreated on her own, birthing many grim personifications of negative forces, including figures such as the Moirai (the Fates), Geras (Old Age), Thanatos (Death), Hypnos (Sleep), Nemesis (Retribution) and Eris (Strife): Strife took after her mother and parthenogenetically produced deities such as Famine or Lawlessness. Other authors and theogonies linked Nyx to other children, with Aeschylus making her mother of the dread Erinyes (Furies). Nyx's branch of the divine family tree remained fiercely independent from other deities: in Hesiod's account, no descendant of Nyx ever had children with a descendant of Earth, a self-enforced genealogical divide.

Something of Nyx's foreboding nature reappears in other Greek texts. In the *Iliad*, Hypnos recalls that he once lulled Zeus to slumber at Hera's behest so that the goddess could torment Heracles; enraged Zeus attempted to hurl Hypnos from heavens, but eventually relented, unwilling to incur the terrible wrath of protective Nyx, "vanquisher of gods and men". Mysterious and unassailable, Nyx was as old as Gaia and, it seems, just as powerful.

Dr. Maciej Paprocki

NOX

CVM LVCE ALTERNAT NOX, VERSIT SIVE SIT ÆSTAS,
SIVE SIT AVTVMNVS, SIVE SIT ACRIS HIEMS.

P. Cand. pinxit. C. G. ab Amling delin. et sculpsit. 1698.

87

Eros (Er)

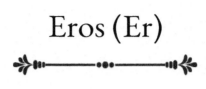

Ἔρως | Ear-oss / Air-oss

Eros was the Greek god of love and desire. In early accounts, Eros is aligned with the primordial gods and is simply the personification of desire. In later accounts, however, Eros is the son of Olympians Aphrodite and Ares, one of a flock of winged gods associated with love and sexual desire known as the Erotes. The iconography of Eros' Roman counterpart, Cupid, remained popular throughout the Medieval and Renaissance periods.

In his *Theogony*, Hesiod writes that Eros is the fourth god to come into existence and describes him as "limb-relaxing Eros, the most beautiful of the immortal gods, who subjugates the mind and sage determinations in the hearts of all gods and all men". His ultimate power to control body and mind is combined with a certain mischievousness, as represented by his emblematic bow and arrows first mentioned by Euripides in *Iphigenia at Aulis*. Often at his mother's request, Eros uses this weapon to make gods and mortals fall in love, with characteristically disastrous and/or humorous consequences. In the Apollo and Daphne myth, Apollo mocks Eros for carrying a weapon he deems inappropriate for a boy; in response, Eros fires a gold tipped arrow at Apollo's chest, filling him with uncontrollable desire for anyone near, then fires a lead tipped arrow at the nearby Daphne, filling her with an intense aversion to love.

Although Eros appears frequently in myth, there are few narratives in which the god himself is a main character rather than a catalyst for others' love. A notable exception is Eros and Psyche: Aphrodite sends Eros to make Psyche fall in love with some hideous creature to punish her for receiving worship for her beauty but, in error, Eros is pierced by his own arrow and falls in love with Psyche.

Adam Thain

Omnia conseruant Eros Anteros; qunia vurgens
Mutuus eterno sedere nectit amor.

His sine nec ratio constat, seqium atq; deorum
Omnia releuntur, ne modus rebus adest.

88

Chronos (Ch)

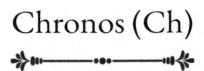

Χρόνος | Cron-oss / Crow-noss

CHRONOS WAS BOTH THE primordial god of time, and the concept of time itself. He was a winged serpent with three heads, each from a different creature: a bull, a lion, and a man. The endless coils of his body were the infinite flow of time in the universe. He was distant from the daily affairs of gods and mortals, but Chronos was still the judge who determined all outcomes eventually.

Chronos was born, or just created, as the third principle in the universe. He was joined by another primordial serpent, Ananke, the goddess and embodiment of necessity. The two gods coiled around one another, mating to create the gods Aither, Chaos, and Erebos.

Between these gods, Chronos and Ananke also created an egg so full of new gods and creations that it split open. The top became Ouranos, and the bottom became Gaia. Then the god Phanes emerged from the egg and set to work creating the rest of the primordial gods. With their work complete, Chronos and Ananke began circling the edges of the cosmos, driving time forward for the universe.

In ancient Greece, Chronos was often mistaken for, or merged with, the Titan Cronos, and the Romans identified both of them with Saturn. Chronos was also often merged with Aion. This led to competing, contradictory, versions of Chronos' mythology, even in antiquity.

Chronos was often depicted as a severe-looking old man with a long grey beard and hair. This version of Chronos is partly the inspiration for modern ideas of "Father Time." In astrology, the planet Saturn, named for the Roman god associated with Chronos, also governs punctuality and accomplishments over time.

Chronos circling the cosmos is also sometimes depicted as the zodiac wheel still used in astrology today.

Trevor Culley

89

Himeros (Ho)

Ἵμερος | Him-eros / He-may-ros

HIMEROS WAS THE LESSER deity of sexual desire and lustful impulses. Depicted as a winged, naked child, he is one of the many *erotes*[1] in the train of Aphrodite. In the seventh century BCE, the poet Hesiod mentions Himeros as a brother and companion to Eros (Love) and Anteros (Requited Love).

Homer talks about the "sweet himeros" electrifying the attraction between Paris and Helen of Troy upon their first meeting, using the name of the puerile god as a noun.

Himeros was never worshipped like a proper deity on his own. Despite his minor status as a divinity, Himeros had power over all mortal creatures and nearly all the immortal ones. Only Athena, Artemis, and Hestia were capable of resisting him. For instance, it was Himeros who moved Zeus to abduct Ganymede.

Himeros was also one of the "secret weapons" of Aphrodite. When she wanted Hera to seduce Zeus, she had her put on her own girdle, thereby arousing "sweet himeros" in Zeus and convincing him to sleep with his wife for a change. No small feat, indeed.

Himeros, virtually identical in his depictions with all the other *erotes*, was a child because he was impetuous and capricious. He was winged because he was fleeting, especially when gratified.

To the Greeks, this did not make him any less divine. Sexual attraction, even though driven by a desire for pleasure, often served a cosmic purpose. Many heroes and demigods were born as a result of the intervention of Himeros.

In modern Greek, Himeros is best expressed in the colloquial noun "kapsùra", which denotes a burning sexual attraction that trumps all else. It is an emotional state distinct from affectionate love (agàpe) and being in love (èrotas). Thus, Himeros is still alive and well in the land of his birth.

Marios Koutsoukos

90

Thalassa (Tl)

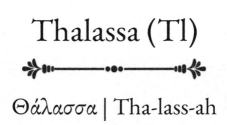

Θάλασσα | Tha-lass-ah

THE DIVINE FEMALE PERSONIFICATION of the sea, Thalassa, originated in Greek myth as the Mediterranean given form. She was a primordial goddess, born from Aether (Bright Sky) and Hemera (Day), and appeared as the sea itself as often as she did a matronly figure. This is appropriate, considering she shares her name with the ancient Greek word for the sea, Θάλασσα, *thalassa*.

Thalassa was the mother of Aphrodite, who was born of the frothing sea-foam and Ouranos' castrated genitals. Together with Pontus, her male counterpart, she also birthed the fish of the sea. One tradition claims that she was also the mother of the Telchines, a group of monstrous blacksmiths who crafted the very sickle that Cronos used to castrate Ouranos!

She was prayed to by sailors wishing for swift winds and safe journeys, though she blamed the winds for her dangerous reputation, claiming that she was calm by nature but became enraged when they lashed against her. The Mediterranean winds and storms could be very dangerous and unpredictable, particularly in winter, and so the worship of deities of the sea was common practice.

She survived long into the Roman period, reflecting the continued importance and centrality of the sea. The most famous depiction of Thalassa is from a fifth century CE mosaic in Antioch, Turkey, where she is depicted with crab-claw horns poking out from wild sea-green hair, draped in seaweed and shells, wielding an oar, and accompanied by dolphins and a dog – elements that appear on other sea deities and personifications, like Pontus, Neptune, Amphitrite, and Scylla.

Thalassa was commonly conflated with the Mediterranean itself, her male counterpart Pontus, and Neptune's queen, Amphitrite. Modern Greek still calls a sea 'thalassa', and one of Neptune's moons is also named after her.

Jessica McKenzie

The Trojan War

THE WAR BETWEEN THE Greek city states and Troy (in the north west of modern-day Turkey) bridges the territories of myth and history. Archaeological discoveries suggest that a great war – or possibly a series of great wars – occurred at Troy. In the telling of the story by Homer known as the *Iliad* (Ilion was one name given to Troy by the Greeks) gods and mortals take sides against one another, and personal grudges and petty grievances push a story of warring armies into a realm of gods and goddesses helping and punishing mortals and immortals alike. It is simultaneously epic and intensely personal.

The cast of the story is enormous, and estimates suggest that more than a thousand different people are mentioned in the poem, and at least a hundred of those contribute directly to the action.

In simple terms, the Greek armies sailed to Troy to capture Helen of Sparta, whom Paris of Troy had escaped with. The armada intended to recapture the queen, and raze Troy to the ground. However, a long stalemate soon set in, with the Greek forces camped on the beaches of Troy, and a siege lasted there for ten years, until Odysseus proposed the idea of constructing a wooden horse...

While primarily a story about war, it is also a record of ancient views of friendship, love, betrayal, valour, marriage, family, and almost every other human emotion.

It has endured for nearly three thousand years because it speaks to people, regardless of the age in which they live, and reveals seemingly eternal truths about what humans are, and possibly always were.

Paris (Pa)

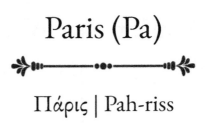

Πάρις | Pah-riss

THE SON OF KING Priam and Queen Hecuba of Troy, Paris (also called Alexander, meaning 'defender of men') was best known to the ancient Greeks for his role in causing the Trojan War.

Before Paris' birth, Hecuba dreamt that she gave birth to a fire torch. Believing this to be an ill omen, Hecuba and Priam ordered a shepherd to abandon the baby Paris on Mount Ida. However, Paris survived after being suckled by a she-bear and was then raised by the shepherd.

Paris was later chosen by Zeus to decide who should receive the golden apple of Eris (goddess of discord), who had said that the apple was for the most beautiful goddess. Athena, Hera, and Aphrodite each claimed the apple and bribed Paris to give it to them, but Aphrodite won after promising Paris the most beautiful woman in the world: Helen, Queen of Sparta.

Paris' identity as a Trojan prince was revealed after he won several matches in the athletic games founded by Hecuba in his memory. On a diplomatic mission to Sparta, Paris met and fell in love with Helen. When Helen's husband Menelaus left Sparta to attend a funeral, Paris either kidnapped Helen or she voluntarily ran away with him, which caused the Greeks to attack Troy.

The ancient Greeks saw Paris as cowardly and unmanly, reflecting Greek attitudes towards the East, since he was very beautiful, fought with a bow, and was rescued by Aphrodite after being defeated by Menelaus in a duel. He did, however, kill Achilles – but only with Apollo's help.

Paris' name possibly comes from the word 'pera' ('bag'), referring to the bag in which he was carried by the shepherd as a baby. He is not the namesake of the French capital, which derives its name from the Gallic Parisii tribe.

Charlotte Gregory

93

Hecuba (Hu)

❧〰〰〰❧

Ἑκάβη | Heck-you-bah

THE DIGNIFIED QUEEN OF ill-fated Troy, wife of King Priam, mother of nineteen of his children, and daughter of the Phrygian king, Hecuba was a beloved matron figure to her people both before and after the Fall of Troy. Her story has been inscribed into mythic history by the poets and dramatists of ancient Greece.

Her stately stature is often contrasted with the humbling bereavement of her children and the austere enslavement she is forced to endure at the hands of her Greek captors. While Troy is besieged by the Greeks, Hecuba prays in the Temple of Athena with the Trojan women and pleads with her son Hector to not fight the Myrmidian hero Achilles, actions which were ultimately in vain. She witnesses the slaughter of Hector and Priam, the sacrifice of her daughter Polyxena on the altar of Achilles' tomb, and the enslavement of her daughters and countrywomen. She is able to avenge the murder of her youngest son, Polydorus, at the hands of the treacherous King Polymestor by blinding him and killing his children.

Though burdened with immense loss, Hecuba escapes her final humiliation through her transformation into a dog. Ancient authors don't agree on the location of this event; some say her change happened as she leapt from her captor's ship; others say that she took her beastly form while still in Troy. It was generally held that the region in which her metamorphosis occurred bore the name 'Cynossema'[1] in remembrance of the tragic queen.

Sierra P. Jones

124. *Hecuba Polymneſtori oculos eruit.*

94

Menelaus (Ml)

❖⫘⸻•◦•⸻⫘❖

Μενέλαος | Men-eh-lay-us

MENELAUS WAS THE SON of Atreus, the brother of Agamemnon and king of Sparta. He was married to the most beautiful woman in the world, Helen.

A prominent figure in the stories about the Trojan War, he fought for the Greeks and helped secure a victory against the city of Troy. After the war, he spent some time lost at sea, wandering between different countries such as Egypt, before returning home to his wife.

Readers from modern and ancient times will know him mostly for the abduction of his wife Helen. She was taken by the Trojan prince Paris after the latter paid a visit to Sparta. Menelaus then gathered support in Greece with the help of his brother and started a war that would last ten years to get her back, ultimately succeeding.

In the modern world, we often see him depicted as fairly weak and tragic, such as in the 2004 film *Troy*, where his wife fell in love with Paris and willingly left Menelaus behind. Menelaus then had to beg his brother for help, and was killed off rather early by Hector. He is thus often remembered as a weak and feeble man who lived in the shadow of his brother.

However, the narrative of the *Iliad* makes it clear that this more modern reputation is far from the truth, and that Menelaus was something else entirely. He is depicted in the epic poem as someone who is known for his willingness to do battle, but also as a sensitive ruler who cared about his fellow Achaeans[1].

Menelaus was one of the Greeks hiding in the wooden horse that was gifted to Troy.

Dries Cuykx

95

Priam (Pr)

❧ ⊷————•••————⊶ ❧

Πρίαμος | Pree-am / Pry-am

THE ANCIENT GREEKS KNEW Priam as the king of Troy at the time of the Trojan War, and father, most notably, to Hector, Paris, and Cassandra.

He features in Homer's *Iliad* as an old man, tall and godlike in appearance, with a kindly disposition. He reassures Helen that he does not blame her for bringing war to his shores. Priam is also recognised for his integrity, as his trustworthiness makes him the Greek leaders' man of choice to ratify the truce oaths ahead of the duel between Paris and Menelaus.

This is not a trait he inherited from his father, however. Podarces, as Priam was formerly known, was the son of double-crossing King Laomedon, whose actions almost cost the prince his freedom, as Heracles pursued retribution for the Trojan ruler's treachery. According to later tradition, his sister offered Heracles the golden veil from her head in exchange for Podarces' liberty. The ransom was accepted and he was installed on the throne bearing his new name, Priam, supposedly derived from the Greek for "to buy".

In the *Iliad*, it is an act of ransom that King Priam is most known for when he journeys into the Achaean camp at great personal risk to negotiate the return of Hector's body from Achilles, the man who had slain so many of his sons. In a poignant scene that has inspired artists through the ages, Priam clasps Achilles' knees in supplication, imploring him to think of his own father and take pity on an old man in his grief. His words stir the heart of the great warrior who accepts Priam's gifts and allows him to carry Hector back to the city.

In wider mythology, Priam's story ends when he is killed by Achilles' son, Neoptolemus, during the final sack of Troy.

King Priam is the titular character of a 1960s opera composed by Sir Michael Tippett.

Emily Small

96

Helen (H)

❧━━━━━━━━━━━❧

Ἑλένη | Hel-en / Hel-en-ee

To the ancient Greeks, Helen took on several personae, most famous however, is her title of most beautiful woman in the world. Helen was seen as the ultimate prize, as well as the scourge of Greece, having 'caused' the mythical Trojan War.

Helen was born to Queen Leda and King Tyndareus of Sparta; however, some sources place her as the child of Zeus and Nemesis. She was first married to Menelaus, Prince of Mycenae, and together they had a daughter, Hermione. Upon the death of Menelaus' father, Helen met Paris, Prince of Troy. There are many divergent mythologies, however the popular theory is that Helen and Paris fell in love and abandoned Sparta (along with Helen's husband and child), and fled to Troy with all her wealth, subsequently wedding and causing the Trojan war. The Kings of Greece set sail for Troy, waging war against the Trojans for 10 years in retaliation. Eventually, the war was won by the Greeks, and Helen returned to Sparta as Queen with her husband Menelaus.

Helen's mythology is contested entirely, with differing versions of almost all aspects of her story being told, from her abduction or elopement, to her murder or peaceful death. She was not only restricted to appearances in mythology, but also in the religious realm, with at least three cults of Helen attested to within the literary record, and archaeological evidence of the Hero cult of Helen and Menelaus in Sparta.

Helen is a polarising figure, she is simultaneously praised and berated, and is impossible to categorise. However, her prevailing beauty and mythology have inspired numerous works throughout history.

Helen was said to have had magical powers as a demigod, from saving sailors at sea, to blinding poets for writing damaging material about her.

Alexia Burrows Charalambidou

H·M ARMSTONG°

97

Odysseus (Oy)

Ὀδυσσεύς O-diss-ee-us

ODYSSEUS, KING OF ITHACA,[1] was best known as the title character of Homer's epic *The Odyssey*, recounting his difficult journey home following the Trojan War. He is described by Homer as cunning and complex; qualities which set him apart from more traditional heroes.

Odysseus was born to Laertes and Anticlea, and married Penelope, who bore a son, Telemachus.[2] As king of Ithaca, Odysseus joined the Trojan War and assisted in taking Troy through his theft of the Palladium,[3] and his plan to use the Trojan Horse. While his cunning may have endeared him to modern audiences, to the Greeks, such wily ways were considered less than heroic. Odysseus' favoured weapon was the bow – the weapon of a coward, who strikes from afar.

Following the Trojan War, Odysseus embarked on a long and troubled journey home – one which saw him defeat enemies such as the cyclops Polyphemus, the sorceress Circe, and the sirens. He was trapped on the island of Ogygia with the nymph Calypso, and visited the underworld, speaking with the spirits of heroes such as Achilles and Heracles. Upon returning to Ithaca, Odysseus, assisted by Telemachus, slaughtered the suitors who were competing for Penelope's hand in marriage.

The Romans knew Odysseus as Ulysses and considered him a trickster – an enemy of their hero Aeneas. Virgil refers to him as 'cruel Odysseus' and portrays him as the opposite of Roman values of duty and honour.

We get the word 'odyssey' from Homer's poem about Odysseus – it has come to mean a long or eventful journey or voyage.

Louise O'Brien

98

Hector (Hh)

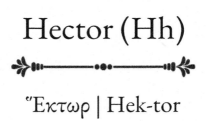

Ἕκτωρ | Hek-tor

HECTOR WAS KNOWN ACROSS the ancient world as the mightiest champion of Troy, in Homer's *Iliad*.

The eldest son of Hecuba and the Trojan king, Priam, Hector was his father's greatest warrior, leading troops in battle and personally duelling with numerous Greek heroes, such as the Greater Ajax. His martial valour stands in contrast to his brother, Paris, whom Hector admonished for cowardice against the Spartan king Menelaus.

Hector's devotion to duty exposed him to grave danger, though. In their final exchange, Hector's wife, Andromache, begged him to avoid combat, but he replied that he would be ashamed to. In a poignant display of humanity before departing, Hector removed his helm and kissed his infant son, Astyanax, when the child was frightened at the sight of his father in armour.

Andromache's greatest fear would come to pass before long. During later fighting, Hector provoked the wrath of Achilles by killing his close companion, Patroclus, triggering a violent rampage that would end with Hector's death.

Hector's final moments simultaneously reveal his dutifulness and fallibility. He alone remained outside Troy's walls to face Achilles, but initially retreated. Abandoned by the gods, Hector was tricked by Athena into fighting. The duel itself was frenetic until Hector was speared in the neck. The enraged Achilles then abused Hector's corpse, dragging it behind his chariot. Only a secret visit from Priam later calmed Achilles, who eventually returned Hector's body.

Hector features at various points in later literature and media. In Dante's *Inferno*, for example, he is found among virtuous non-Christians in Limbo. More recently, he was played by Eric Bana in *Troy* (2004), opposite Brad Pitt's Achilles, although the film takes egregious liberties with the Homeric plot!

Dr. Alex Imrie

Hector
troianus

Nicola. de. Br fecit Fransoÿs van Beusecom excudit 120

99

Aeneas (As)

❦•••————•••————•••❦

Αἰνείας | Eh-nee-as / Ah-nee-us / Uh-nay-us

I N THE ANCIENT GREEK literary tradition, Aeneas was a child of the goddess Aphrodite and the mortal Anchises. The Homeric Hymn to Aphrodite describes the circumstances of their meeting, where Zeus had caused the goddess to become infatuated with Anchises in retribution, as she had caused Zeus to desire mortal women first. Anchises is promised protection from the gods' wrath so long as he keeps his affair with Aphrodite a secret. Naturally, as a mortal, he brags about it later, and is rewarded with a thunderbolt to the foot from Zeus, leaving him disabled.

His demigod son, Aeneas, goes on to feature as a minor character in the Iliad, fighting on the side of Troy in the Trojan War. Aeneas was described as a formidable fighter, but despite his bravery, he was overpowered by two notable Greeks on the battlefield due to their pure strength. His mother, Aphrodite, and Apollo saved him from the duel with Diomedes after he had been seriously injured, healing him before he returned to the fighting. The gods saved him again when he met Achilles in battle, for though Aeneas had divine blood as well, there was no chance that he could defeat Achilles. Poseidon rescued Aeneas at that moment, claiming that he was fated to survive and later become the king of the Trojans in the future.

Much of Aeneas's life after the Trojan War is not described by the Greeks, but by the Roman poet Vergil in the *Aeneid*. Vergil writes of the escape from Troy, with Aeneas carrying his father Anchises away from the city with his son Ascanius, and their subsequent travels across the Mediterranean. The Trojans eventually came to settle in Italy and found Lavinium, whose descendants go on to found Alba Longa, and later, Rome.

Aidan Mooney

F. Boucher Pinx.

P.F. Courtois Sculp.

Venus & Enée.

A Paris chés Buldet, rue de Gervois.

100

Ajax (Aj)

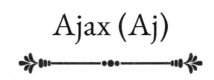

Αἴας | Ay-jax / Eye-as / Eye-ax

BEFORE MAKING HIS NAME during the Trojan War, Ajax's family line provided some tough acts to follow. His divinely-favoured grandfather built the walls of Ilium[1] alongside the gods themselves, his Argonaut father formed the vanguard in Heracles' sack of the city, and prophecy stated Troy couldn't fall without his cousin Achilles.

Ajax was blessed at birth by Heracles and draped in the hero's lion skin cloak. The touch of the cloak made Ajax's skin impervious, leaving only his armpits vulnerable. Once fully grown, Ajax was powerful, well-built, and towered over others. In battle he carried a huge shield made of seven layers of ox hide under which his archer half-brother, Teucer, sheltered between loosing arrows from his bow.

Considered second only to Achilles, once his cousin retired, Ajax became the preeminent warrior with the epithet 'Bulwark of the Greeks'. Ajax doesn't strictly have an aristeia[2] in the Iliad, taking more of a defensive role, but is easily one of the most powerful characters: fighting Hector in single combat, battling to protect the Greek's ships, single-handedly holding off the enemy, and recovering the bodies of Patroclus and Achilles.

Ajax's need to prove himself though, opened the way for deadly hubris. He rejected Athena's aid, declaring himself capable of holding the line. When the prize of Achilles' armour was awarded to Odysseus, Ajax's sense of rejection and failure was too great. Seeking revenge on those he saw as responsible, whether by Athena's interference or simple clouded judgement, he slaughtered livestock in a fit of rage. Discovering his transgression and to escape his shame, he disappeared to a secluded place and fell on his sword, piercing through his armpit. From the drops of blood that fell, flowers are said to have sprung up with the letters *ai* painted on their petals – the sound of Ajax's grief and an echo of his name.

Vicki Feltham

Aiax in florem migrat, dum se opprimit ira,
Hanc illi ostendunt arma negata viam.

Der Ajax selbst den tod sich fügt,
Weil ihm sein will nicht wird vergnügt.

101

Patroclus (Pt)

❧———••———❧

Πάτροκλος | Pat-rock-luss / Pat-roh-kloss

THE COMPANION OF THE ancient Greek hero Achilles, Patroclus stands out among the characters portrayed in the writings of Homer for his contradictions: a heroic warrior who is renowned for his kindness. His death prompts the return of Achilles to fighting, and so is the catalyst for the triumph of the Greek army over the city of Troy.

Patroclus is thought to mean "the glory" (kleos) of the father (pater), but while he is young, he kills another child and is given away by his father Menoetius. King Peleus raises him with his own son Achilles, whose mother, the goddess Thetis, is absent. In Homer's account, Patroclus is referred to as older than Achilles, and it is indicated that he was a role-model for him.

In the Trojan war, Patroclus borrows the armour of Achilles in order to inspire the troops and he fights bravely. He is warned not to go too far, for it is not his destiny to conquer the city, but he becomes dazed after encountering the god Apollo in battle, and the armour is taken from him. His true identity is discovered, and he is killed, arguing with the Trojan prince Hector to the last, and prophesying that Achilles will soon triumph.

The other Greek heroes defend and rescue the body of Patroclus, and Achilles and the others mourn him. The ghost of Patroclus visits Achilles asking that their bones rest together after death. Funeral games are held for Patroclus to honour him.

There is deep affection between Achilles and Patroclus, speaking of love, embracing, and their suffering when they can no longer be together, and many have interpreted this as a sexual relationship.

Patroclus is someone in whom Achilles can confide, and there is an element of teasing between them, where Achilles compares Patroclus to a toddler trailing after a mother.

Allison Menai Newbould

102

Achilles (Ll)

❧⊱————•••————⊰❧

Ἀχιλλεύς | Ah-kil-eez / Uh-kil-eez

ACHILLES IS A HERO known as the 'Greatest of all Greeks' for the instrumental role he played in the Trojan War. He was the son of Peleus, ruler of Phthia, and the Nereid, Thetis. His role in the Trojan War is exemplified in Homer's *Iliad*, even being the subject of the poem's first line. Achilles grew up in Phthia alongside his companion Patroclus. Both Achilles and Patroclus were educated by the centaur Chiron, as was traditional for heroes of their time. It is said that to make her son invincible, Thetis dipped him into the river Styx holding him up by the heel, leaving his heel as Achilles' only vulnerability.

In terms of the *Iliad*, Achilles is best known due to his rage, specifically around Hector's death. Achilles refused to fight due to a dispute with the Greek army's commander, Agamemnon. After days of battles the Greeks were losing their morale without Achilles in the field. Seeing this, Patroclus put on his companion's armour and went off to battle only to be slain by Hector. After learning of this Achilles flew into a rage, chasing Hector through the battlefield, and although Hector tried to run away, beating swift-footed Achilles in a race was no joke. Achilles was slain by Paris towards the end of the Trojan War using an arrow guided by Apollo. In the Underworld, when he met Odysseus, he mentioned he would prefer to be an alive serf than the King of all the lifeless dead who surrounded him.

Achilles represents the inevitability of fate, the brutal reality of heroism, and the loss that comes alongside it. For the beauty of life is not in glory, but in living.

Alexander the Great himself found Achilles a huge source of inspiration, and was known to visit Achilles' tomb.

Sol A. Cardenas

Gavinus Hamilton Pinxit.   Achilles vents his rage on Hector.   Achilles in exanimem Hectora sævit

Published at Map 17.99 by LAURIE & WHITTLE, 53 Fleet Street, London.

Olympians

HIGH ON MOUNT OLYMPUS, these gods and goddesses ruled over the human world of men, but they were not passive observers. Every Olympian god finds their way into the myths of men, helping them, hindering them, rewarding them and punishing them.

They were the third generation of gods, after the Primordial deities and the Titans. A war between the Titans and the Olympians (the Titanomachy) raged for ten years before the Olympians achieved victory, imprisoning in Tartarus those Titans who threatened their power.

This group of twelve* – the dodecatheon – existed in contrast to the Chthonic deities, and governed the lives of living mortals.

Unlike many later religions, the Greek gods did not want to be loved by mortals, but they insisted upon being respected and worshipped. Not to do so was to risk the wrath of these sometimes capricious, bad-tempered, jealous, and vindictive deities.

While capable of breathtaking acts of benevolence and creativity, the Olympains also showed the worst of our behaviours, making them complex, and occasionally infuriating, characters.

*Dionysus has been moved to Dramatis Personae in order to keep the number here to the canonical twelve, although he is of course one of the Olympians. Similarly, Hades has been categorised with the Chthonic characters, though as the brother of Zeus and Poseidon he is sometimes considered an Olympian.

Zeus (Z)

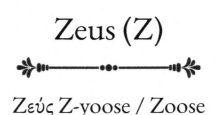

Ζεύς Z-yoose / Zoose

To the ancient Greeks, Zeus was the cloud-bringer, the thunder god, and the king of the gods who resided in a palace at the summit of Mount Olympus. Armed with thunderbolts, and enslaved by his worst impulses, Zeus was a distinctly anthropomorphised[1] kind of deity, one that reflected humanity in all its majestic and flawed ways, filled with powers and peccadillos.

Zeus was born of the titans Cronus and Rhea, the sixth child after Hestia, Demeter, Hera (later his wife), Hades, and Poseidon. It had been prophesied that Cronus would be brought down by his own children, and so he adopted a policy of eating his progeny[2] to prevent the oracle's[3] fulfilment. Rhea, anguished at the cannibalism of her partner, planned to save Zeus by switching the newborn god with a large rock wrapped in swaddling blankets, which Cronus swallowed believing it to be his son.

After growing up on the island of Crete, Zeus poisoned his father into vomiting up his siblings, before releasing the dreaded Hecatoncheires and the Cyclopes. A war between the younger gods – the Olympians – and the old gods – the Titans – erupted. Fulfilling the prophecy, as all prophecies must be fulfilled, Zeus led the victory of the young gods, afterwards imprisoning the old ones across the ancient world.

The Romans knew Zeus as Jupiter or Jove, and he was associated with many of the facets of his Greek fore-runner, including the role as father (Jupiter itself derives from early Latin words *Iou-Pater*, literally "sky father") and head of the state. Obviously, Jupiter is also the name of the planet, and people born under this planet were reputed to be cheerful babies.

Another name for Jupiter used by the Romans was Jove, hence our modern word, jovial.

George Connor

IVPPITER

Polidorus inue.   HG. sculp. 6

105

Poseidon (Po)

❧⊢•••——•••——••⊣❧

Ποσειδῶν | Poss-eye-don

POSEIDON WAS THE SON of the Titans Kronos and Rhea, and the brother of Zeus, Hades, Hera, Demeter, and Hestia. The sea was Poseidon's realm – he was famous for his ability to manipulate ocean waves and his capacity to bring forth storms and earthquakes (plus, perhaps strangely, his dominion over horses). You'll often see him depicted with a trident, sometimes on a chariot and surrounded by sea-life both real (fish) and less real (Nereids).

Poseidon is represented in the earliest available literature – most often as a character plagued with a raging temper that sometimes bordered on the contradictory. During the Trojan War, in which Greeks laid siege to the city of Troy, he intervened on behalf of the Greeks. And yet, during the very same conflict, he spoke venomous words into the ear of Agamemnon concerning Achilles, the Greeks' greatest hero. After the War, he plagued Odysseus with multiple obstacles as this *other* great Greek hero tried to get home. Admittedly, Poseidon was inspired here by Odysseus' blinding of Poseidon's son, the Cyclops Polyphemus, but these examples go to show the god's inherent temperamentality.

Poseidon got a rebrand as Neptune under the Romans, and both 'versions' have enjoyed a long life in art and culture. You'll find him in paintings, plays, literature, films, and video games too: his name is used to denote adventures at sea (as in the title of the film *The Poseidon Adventure* (1972)), and he's the blueprint for many fantastical undersea kings including Triton in Disney's *The Little Mermaid* (1989). You can side with him in the strategy game *Age of Mythology* (2002) or even poke out his eyes in *God of War III* (2010).[1]

Ross Clare

106

Athena (A)

‗‗‗‗‗‗‗‗‗‗‗‗‗‗‗‗‗‗

Ἀθήνη | Ah-thee-nah / Ah-thee-nee

FOR THE ANCIENT GREEKS, the goddess Athena played an enormous role in their private and civic lives. Her dominion over wisdom, strategic war, and weaving made her the object of worship by a wide array of people. Typically, she was depicted as a woman and warrior, armed with a helmet, spear, and *aegis* decorated with the head of Medusa. Her symbols include the owl, the olive tree, and snakes. Athena is also regarded as a virgin goddess. Today, Athena is often vaunted as a symbol of reason, democracy, wisdom, and is a somewhat controversial icon.

Even amongst the Olympians, Athena's birth was quite extraordinary. In one of the most widely-known origin myths, Zeus impregnated the goddess of wisdom, Metis. Zeus feared a prophecy that said the children of Metis would be more powerful than him, and he hastily swallowed Metis. Soon, however, he began to experience terrible headaches. At once, Hephaestus was summoned to split open Zeus' head to relieve the pain. Upon doing so, Athena sprang from Zeus' head in adult form and fully armed. Many regarded Athena as Zeus' favourite child as she would often carry out his will.

Athena's exploits and tales of aiding heroes are abundant. One story relates how, during the War of the Giants, Athena skinned the giant Pallas in order to fashion her *aegis*. She is also known to have come to the aid of Odysseus, Heracles, and Perseus.

Perhaps her most famous connection is to the city of Athens, from which she likely received her name. She became the patron of the city after offering the Athenians an olive tree in a contest with Poseidon. At the Acropolis overlooking the city, there were temples and statues dedicated to the various forms of Athena, including Athena Polias[1] and Athena Parthenos[2], the latter of which gives the Parthenon its name, and where we get the term parthenogenesis[3].

Keeli Cadwell

18. *Inuidiæ sedes, et luce carentia regna*   *Mandat inulta poli ne sydera spectet Aglauros*
    Mersa chao informi torua Minerua subit.   *Illa deæ magnæ iussa repente facit.*

107

Artemis (At)

Ἄρτεμις | Ar-teh-miss

FAR-SHOOTING ARTEMIS, ONE OF the twelve Olympians, was born to Zeus and Leto on the island of Delos. The first-born twin of Apollo, she assisted her mother with the birth of her brother, and so was worshipped as the goddess of childbirth. As Apollo was god of the Sun, his twin sister Artemis was goddess of the Moon.

Artemis was a fierce huntress, and as a youth she asked her father, the loud-thundering Zeus, that she keep her maidenhood – and so Artemis became the virgin huntress, spending her days roaming the mountains and woodlands of Crete with her company of Oceanids (freshwater nymphs) and Oreads (mountain nymphs).

But Artemis was also vengeful, and one fateful recipient of Artemis' wrath was Actaeon, who, whilst separated from his hunting party, stumbled across Artemis bathing in a sacred grove. Her attending nymphs tried to shield her from the eyes of the Boeotian stranger, but Artemis stood tall above them, exposed. As she was unarmed, Artemis cupped the water from the spring and sprinkled it onto Actaeon's head, daring him to speak of what he had seen. But before he could say a word, he was transformed into a stag, growing horns, hooves, and hair all over. Fleeing from the naked goddess, he was hunted down and ripped apart by his own hounds.

Artemis was worshipped across the Mediterranean in different forms – as the watcher of harbours, as the protector of women and girls, as the mistress of wild animals, and of fertility. Her worship was prominent at Ephesus (in present-day Turkey), where a vast temple was constructed in her honour. The Temple of Artemis at Ephesus was so magnificent, it became one of the Seven Wonders of the Ancient World.

Lucy Neill

Boulogne Pinx.   Sornique Sculp.

ACTÉON PETIT FILS DE CADMUS METAMORPHOSÉ EN CERF.

Acteon devoré par sa meute en Fureur,   Pour avoir un moment contemplé tes appas,
Diane, ne scauroit que fletrir ton honneur   Ne devoit-ce pas être une assez rude peine
Et t'attirer les noms d'injuste, d'inhumaine   Que de les avoir vus, et de n'en jouir pas?

a Paris chez charpentier rue S.Jacque au Coq.

Moraine.

108

Aphrodite (Ah)

━━━◆●━━━━━●●●━━━━━●◆━━━

Ἀφροδίτη | A-fro-die-tee / A-fro-dee-tee

BORN FROM THE OCEAN, as delicate as pearl, and sharp as a rose thorn – Aphrodite was known to the ancient Greeks as the goddess of love, beauty, desire, and sex. She was likely introduced to the Greek pantheon from the near East, taking influence from goddesses like Ishtar[1] and Astarte.[2]

Aphrodite's birth was as mystical and ethereal as the goddess herself; she rose fully formed from the seafoam created after Ouranos' castrated genitals fell into the ocean. She eventually washed up on the shore of Kythera, which later became an important cult centre for her worship.

It was Zeus who chose Aphrodite's husband, and he married her off to his son Hephaestus. Less than pleased with this decision, Aphrodite took on several lovers outside of her marriage – most notably, the god Ares. Hephaestus once laid a clever trap for his wife and Ares by trapping them in an indestructible net during one of their trysts, leaving them to be ridiculed by their fellow Olympians.

Aphrodite was the victor of the so-called Judgement of Paris, one of the events which led to the Trojan War. The Trojan prince Paris was selected to choose between three goddesses, all of whom were vying for a golden apple which declared them "the fairest." Aphrodite won the contest after offering Paris the hand of the most beautiful woman in the world, but failed to mention that Helen of Sparta was already married.

Her Roman counterpart is Venus, who similarly held dominion over love, fertility, and beauty. Venus was notable in the Roman pantheon for being the mother of Aeneas,[3] whom later Roman nobility declared descendancy from.

Aphrodite's most famous artistic rendition is The Birth of Venus by Sandro Botticelli, which depicts Aphrodite's fantastical birth from the sea.

Regina Nagan

VENVS

Parce metu Cytherea, favet tibi & annuit uni,   Et nunc Sigæo clafsem de littore folvit:
   Promifsæq; Helenæ flagrat amore Paris.   Heu, quantum Phrygii sanguinis illa vehet!

109

Hermes (He)

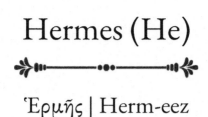

Ἑρμῆς | Herm-eez

B ORN OF ZEUS AND Maia, the Greek god Hermes was the messenger of the gods. Usually depicted with his characteristic winged sandals and hat, Hermes moved incredibly fast to deliver important messages. Zeus, for instance, sent Hermes to Poseidon to forbid him from flooding Attica after it was decided that Athena would be the first to found a city there.

Hermes was only just born when he invented the lyre, by attaching a set of strings to the shell of a tortoise he found. Later on the same day, he cleverly stole the cattle of his brother Apollo, the god of music. When Zeus learned of the matter, he laughed at the newborn's cunning. Hermes gave the lyre to Apollo, and in turn received Apollo's staff, the 'caduceus', with which Hermes is often represented.

Hermes also had various other tasks and domains. He was the patron of merchants, traders, thieves, herds, and more. Additionally, he performed the task of the 'psychopomp', the guide of the souls of the deceased into the Underworld. It is described, for example, how Hermes guided the souls of Penelope's suitors to Hades after Odysseus killed them upon his return to Ithaca.

In Rome, Hermes was known as Mercury. In fact, the English word 'mercurial' ('volatile', 'unpredictable') derives from him. He also lent his Roman name to the planet closest to the sun in our solar system. The main postal service in Greece, the Hellenic Post, still uses the visage of the god in their logo, as a reference to the mythological messenger. Several contemporary superheroes were also inspired by Hermes and his speed: DC Comics' The Flash (who also wore winged sandals) was, for instance, originally described as "the reincarnation of the winged Mercury"[1]!

Alexander Vandewalle

MERCVRIVS

110

Hera (Ha)

$\clubsuit$═══════•••═══════$\clubsuit$

Ἥρη | Hee-reh / Hair-ah

HELP FRIENDS, HARM ENEMIES: Hera followed this ancient Greek moral precept more devotedly than many others. Under her protection, cities could flourish, successful marriages might be made, and the universe flourished in her guise as the feminine principle of sovereignty. Her fecundity enhanced the natural world, too, by causing a meadow to bloom as she made love with Zeus, her brother and husband.

That marriage had been made after Zeus overthrew their father, Cronos. Cronos had sought to prevent any child usurping him by swallowing each after they were born. But Hera, like others of her siblings, was reborn from her father's mouth after Zeus allied with their mother, Rhea, and fed Cronos an emetic drug.

Hera had three children with Zeus: the warrior, Ares, the birthing goddess Eilithyia, and Hebe, the personified Youth. Another child, the craft god Hephaestus, was variously regarded as Hera's son by Zeus or Hera's alone, conceived in her fury at the appearance from Zeus' head of Athena, his child by the swallowed (that motif again) Titan Metis.

A further child of Hera (or according to some sources the Earth goddess, Gaia) was also conceived in anger at Zeus. This was Typhon, created to usurp Zeus but blasted apart by Zeus' thunderbolt.

As well as conceiving children in anger, Hera's fury was directed towards Zeus's many sexual partners and their children, notably Heracles, although her drive to harm her stepson ended with his marriage, as a god, to her daughter Hebe.

To the Romans, Hera was associated with the goddess Juno.

In modern reworkings, Hera typically features as a cheated-on wife who resents Zeus's lovers/victims and children, especially Heracles.

In an ironic use of the sacred bird of Hera/Juno, the strutting husband of Juno Doyle is the paycock ('peacock') of Sean o'Casey's Juno and the Paycock, *set in 1920s Dublin.*

Susan Deacy

Io ti ueggio Marito mio ribaldo
e tu fogliosa scapestrata uacca
l'una et l'altro sta pur anch saldo

111

Demeter (Dm)

❧⊪————••⊪————⊪❧

Δημήτηρ | Deh-mee-ter / Duh-mee-ter

To the ancient Greeks, rich-haired Demeter was the Grain Mother, the bringer of seasons and giver of life-sustaining gifts.

Demeter was the second daughter of the Titans Cronus and Rhea, and the sister of Hestia, Hera, Poseidon, Hades, and Zeus. Like her siblings, Demeter was swallowed by Cronus out of fear that they would overthrow him, but was eventually freed by her brother Zeus. Together, they overthrew Cronus and his fellow Titans, and the Olympians became the rulers of the cosmos.

Demeter's best-known myth involves her search for her daughter Persephone, whom Hades abducted and took to the Underworld. It's just before this quest that Demeter, under the guise of an old woman, is given a hospitable reception by the king Celeus. As a reward for his kindness, the goddess decides to make his son Demophon immortal, but cannot complete the ritual. Instead, Demeter teaches his older brother Triptolemus the art of agriculture, and he teaches the rest of Greece how to plant, care for, and harvest crops.

Nine days later, Demeter learns of her daughter's abduction from the sun god Helios, and the goddess is so distraught that all plant life starts dying.

The subsequent famine in the mortal plane compels Zeus to command Hades to release Persephone. However, Hades gives Persephone six pomegranate seeds to eat, binding her to the Underworld for six months each year.

This represented the change of seasons, as vegetation would wither whenever Demeter and her daughter were separated, and flourish when they were reunited.

Demeter and Persephone were central to the Eleusinian Mysteries, a Panhellenic mystery cult held in Eleusis, said to be the site where the goddesses were reunited, with names such as Aeschylus, Plato, Augustus, Hadrian and Marcus Aurelius as known initiates.

Tom Bright

Hic Cererem tectis Phytalus susceperat Heros,
Cui primum sacri largita est semina pomi,
Quod mortale genus FICVM uocat.

Salvator Rosa Inu. scul.

112

Apollo (Ap)

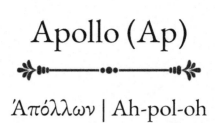

Ἀπόλλων | Ah-pol-oh

APOLLO, SON OF ZEUS and Leto (and twin brother of Artemis), was a complex Olympian deity associated with music, divination, archery, and healing.

Archaeological representations of Apollo depict him as young, beardless, and long-haired, indicative of his eternal youth, and symbolising his role as protector of young men, whose hair he received as an offering to mark their transition to adolescence. Typically, iconographic depictions of Apollo contain symbols such as a lyre,[1] a raven,[2] a wreath and branch of laurel,[3] and a bow and arrows.[4]

Apollo had many sanctuaries across the Mediterranean visited for advice and guidance, including Delphi, Didyma, and Clarus. Here, priests and priestesses of Apollo entered an altered state of mind to access the mind of Apollo, becoming a conduit or direct channel of communication between the god and the inquirer. Some of the most famous seers include Cassandra, Helenus, the Pythia, and the Sybil.

In Homer's *Iliad*, Chryses, a Trojan priest of Apollo, offers a ransom to the Achaeans for his abducted daughter Chryseis, which the commander-in-chief Agamemnon refuses. This was an insult to Chryses' sacred priestly status. Chryses prayed to Apollo for assistance, who, angered by the violation, came down from Olympus, shooting arrows that brought a plague into the Achaean encampment.

Worshippers of Apollo sought aid from Apollo the Healer, and the god was often referred to with the epithet "Iatros", meaning "Doctor". The Romans adopted Apollo from the Greek pantheon as (unlike other Hellenic deities) they had no pre-existing equivalent of their own. The Romans also saw Apollo as a healer, and the Vestal Virgins addressed him as "Apollo Medice" (also meaning "Doctor").

Even today, some medical schools around the world have their graduating physicians undertake the original Hippocratic Oath, which begins, "I swear by Apollo the Healer"

Caitlin Yool

113

Ares (Ar)

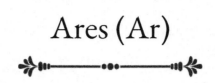

Ἄρης | Air-eez / Ah-reez

ARES WAS ONE OF two Olympians who represented the domain of war. Unlike his half-sister Athena, who represented the strategic side of war, Ares was the embodiment of the chaos, carnage and bloodshed that was typical of warfare. He was also said to represent the necessary qualities and emotions needed to wage war, such as courage and rage. As a result, he was an unpopular deity, both among the gods who lived on Olympus, and to the mortals who worshipped them.

Ares was born to Zeus and Hera, and was the brother of Hephaestus, Hebe and Eileithyia. He remained unmarried, but had numerous children by mortal women, and most famously, carried on an affair with Aphrodite behind the back of her husband, Hephaestus.

Ares appears as a major player in relatively few myths, and in the myths in which he does appear, it is rare that he comes out on top of a situation, in spite of his reputation. In the *Iliad*, for example, the goddess Dione tells a story of how Ares was once captured by the Aloadae giants and trapped in a jar for 13 months. Later in the same poem, Ares is severely wounded by a mortal, Diomedes, and is forced to retire from battle, screaming in agony.

While he was worshipped very little in Greece, the Romans knew and worshipped him as Mars, and he was considered one of their most important gods, especially since the Romans built their empire on war and conquest. It is said that Mars' sons, Romulus and Remus, had founded the eternal city of Rome.

In spite of not being widely worshipped, Ares' influence can still be seen today. The Areopagus hill in Athens was named after him, after he was tried and acquitted for murder there.

Livia Adams

MARS.

114

Hephaestus (Hp)

❖◦═════◦•◦═════◦❖

Ἥφαιστος | Heh-fai-sto

HEPHAESTUS, ALSO KNOWN AS Hephaistos, was the ancient Greek god of artisans, blacksmiths and craftsmen. His mother was Hera, the queen of the gods and wife of Zeus (though we aren't entirely sure if Zeus was his father). In one version of the myth, Hephaestus was born with a disability that limited his movement. Because of this, he was initially rejected by Hera, who threw him down Mount Olympus. He was rescued and raised by Thetis, a Nereid[1] who was also Achilles' mother.

In another version of the myth, Hephaestus attempted to protect Hera from Zeus, and was flung to earth by him as a result. In this version, his disability was a consequence of the fall, and he was raised by the Sintians – famed craftsmen – on the island of Lemnos.

He eventually returned to Olympus accompanied by Dionysos, the god of wine and theatre. Many of the vase representations we have of Hephaestus show him on donkey-back, enjoying his revelry with the Maenads and Satyrs[2] as they make their way back to the sacred mountain.

Once he returned, Hephaestus made many incredible objects, including automata[3] in the shape of young girls that acted as his mobility aids. He also built Achilles' new shield and arms after Hector stole them during the Trojan war, as well as tripods for the gods' dining halls that could move on their own. His skilled craftsmanship made him a vitally important god to artisans, and his temple in Athens was in the Agora, the main market where they sold their wares and had their workshops.

In Roman mythology, Hephaestus' counterpart was Vulcan. His workshop was thought to be below Mount Etna in Sicily, and is why we have the term "volcano" today to describe large mountains that spit fire!

Justin Lorenzo Biggi

VVLCANVS.

Celidorus Inur.   Maltzius sculp.

115

Hestia (Hs)

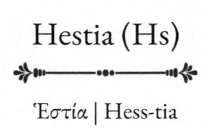

Ἑστία | Hess-tia

To the people of ancient Greece, Hestia was the goddess responsible for domestic life, the hearth, and therefore all oblations[1] on the hearth. This makes her name quite literal, she is the personification of the hearth, fireplace, or altar. In the sacred grounds and temples of other deities, she held some stake in the average man's sacrifice to the gods, accepting her share of honour as the goddess of the sacred sacrificial altar's fire. She lived not only on Mount Olympus, but deep in every home.

After proposals from both Apollo and Poseidon, Hestia devoted herself as a virgin goddess at Zeus' sanctuary. Due to her virginity, she is pictured as a modest, veiled woman. Ancient Greek artists portrayed her holding a nameless floral branch (perhaps of the chaste-tree[2]) or a kettle.

Hestia was Cronus and Rhea's child, alongside Demeter, Hera, Hades, Poseidon, and Zeus. According to myth, when Cronus had eaten his kids in a paranoid fear of them overcoming him, Hestia, being the firstborn (and eaten), was the last to be ejected from her father. Some consider this to render her both the eldest and youngest of the children.

After Zeus led a war against their father and other Titans, as the king of gods, he made Hestia responsible for the feeding of the Olympian hearth from gracious sacrifices. Due to her reputation for this responsibility, mortal people claimed her to be the chief of the goddesses.

Despite being a goddess with limited mythology, it can be said that Hestia has left her own mark on religion and dedication – in and out of the home – right up to the current day. Romans, who knew her as Vesta, lit a fire in Vesta's temple that was maintained by the Vestal Virgins, who dedicated themselves to celibacy, not unlike the goddess herself.

The burning of this fire was said to represent the eternal nature of Rome.

Aiden Cattanach

VESTA

VESTA·P·R· QVIRITIVM

VES TA

Titans

T HESE TWELVE CHILDREN OF the Primordial gods are best identified through the human traits bestowed upon them in stories, which spread widely throughout ancient Greece. Most notable of these was the war with the Olympians.

In some ways, the Titans are an extension of the creativity that began when the Primordial gods emerged from Chaos, inasmuch as they are gods of water, light, intelligence, prophecy, constellations, memory and other concepts, sometimes abstract, sometimes more concrete, which show the increasing complexity of the world as it grew from its fundamental beginnings.

While they were banished to the Underworld, we don't consider them to be Underworld gods in this book, instead showing how they formed part of a chain of ruling orders: the first order was overthrown by the Titans, who were then in turn defeated by the Olympians, who endured as the pantheon of ancient Greek gods.

Cronos (T)

Κρόνος | Cron-oss / Crow-noss

"*TEMPUS EDAX RERUM*"[1] – time, consumer of all things. This sentiment from Ovid's *Metamorphoses* is never more literal than in the mythology surrounding Cronos, the ancient Greek god of time, whose name is the origin of the word 'chronological'.

Cronos was the youngest of the 12 Titan children of Uranus, the god of the sky, and Gaea, the goddess of the earth. He was the King of the Titans and the father of the Olympian gods; Hestia, Demeter, Hera, Hades, Poseidon and Zeus, who he fathered with his wife, sister, and consort, Rhea.

In Greek mythology, Cronos became king by separating the heavens from the earth when he was persuaded by his mother (who was furious with Uranus for locking the Hecatoncheires inside her womb), to castrate his father with a sickle. However, having usurped his own father, Cronos became paranoid about being usurped by his *own* children, so decided to devour his children at birth. His wife Rhea managed to save her youngest son Zeus by hiding him away, and he eventually returned in disguise and tricked Cronos into drinking a potion that made him throw up his other children. This event led to the Titanomachy, the war between gods and Titans. The outcome was the defeat of Cronos and the Titans, which either led to Cronos being imprisoned in Tartarus or forgiven and being made King of Elysium, depending on the version of the myth.

Cronos was mainly worshipped by the pre-Hellenic Greeks and was called Saturn in the Roman version of the mythology. Cronos was also often connected to agriculture with the Kronia[2], which took place in Attica, celebrating the harvest.

Ashleigh Hamilton

118

Crius (Ci)

❖⊱••━━━━•••━━━━••⊰❖

Κριός | Kree-oss / Kree-uss

To the ancient Greeks, Crius (or Krios) was a very old god from 'the golden age'.[1] Crius was a Titan, one of twelve, six sons and six daughters of twhe primordial gods Ouranos (Sky) and Gaia (Earth). Married to his half-sister they had three children: Astraeus, Pallas and Perses, deities associated with stars, warfare and destruction respectively.

Responsible for the constellations, hoCrius was one of four brothers who were the cosmic pillars separating the sky from the earth. He was probably the southern pillar with the connection that Crius translates as 'Ram' and the constellation Aries[2] is the first to appear in the southern sky at the beginning of the Greek year. Constellations were very important to the Greeks as they used constellations and the stars for navigation.

Crius' younger brother, Cronos, conspired to overthrow his father and involved the four pillars, who held Ouranos down while Cronos castrated him with a sickle. Ironically Crius was therefore instrumental in the downfall of the Titans. Not only was an Olympian goddess born from the castration[3] but the prophecy that Cronos' children would overthrow him was set in motion. This prophecy, the ten-year Titanomachy, and the installation of the Olympian gods as permanent rulers, was an important succession myth to the Greeks. Crius, who did not have a specific role in the war, was cast with the other Titans into Tartarus.

The ship, Titanic, because of its size and Titanium, because of its strength, are named after the Titans.

Colin Gough

119

Hyperion (Hy)

❧———◆•——•◦•——•◆———❧

Ὑπερίων Hy-peer-ee-uhn / Hih-peer-ee-on / Hih-pair-ee-on

H E WHO WATCHES FROM above, Hyperion[1], was the son of Gaia, the Earth, and Ouranus, the Sky. It was he who brought light to the world and he who ruled the cycle of night. To the ancient Greeks, he was the one who watched over (some say he created) the harmony of the sun, moon and stars. Being in control of the rising of the sun and as the father of Dawn, he represented the Pillar of East, which was one of the four pillars that held up the sky[2].

Hyperion was married to the Titaness Theia, who was the goddess of sight and also his sister. According to many, this union of heavenly light and the controller of the sun and moon led many to believe that it was this couple that gave humanity the gift of sight. This made Hyperion very well-liked in ancient Greece. Alas, joy cannot last for eternity. In the ten-year Titanomachy, Hyperion was a part of his brother, Cronos', force against the Olympian gods. These new deities banished Cronos' army, including Hyperion, to the depths of Tartarus.

It is a great tragedy that Hyperion does not have many myths associated with him. The times he is mentioned in ancient literature such as Hesiod's *Theogony*, or Homer's *Iliad*, are with reference to his children, Helios[3], Selene[4] and Eos[5].

Even though Hyperion, 'the Observer', may seem a mere brother to the more dynamic Cronos, he has been referenced in more recent pieces of literature. In Elizabethan England, the poem of John Keats, *Hyperion*, reveals his "sov'reignty, and rule, and majesty", and in the 21st century novels, *Percy Jackson and the Olympians*, Hyperion's eyes are described as gold: "like miniature suns".

The world's tallest tree is named after the Titan Hyperion, for they share the quality of being the 'high one', with the tree being 116 metres tall.

Mehr-un-Nisa Syed

120

Iapetus (Ia)

᛭ ᚷᚷᚷ ——————— •• ———————— ᚷᚷᚷ ᛭

Ἰαπετός Ee-ah-pet-oss / Eye-ah-pet-us / Yap-eh-tus / Yap-eh-toss

IAPETUS, TO THE ANCIENT Greeks, was one of the original twelve Titan gods and was a son of Ouranos and Gaia. Along with four of his Titan brothers, when Ouranos forced himself onto Gaia, Iapetus held his father down whilst Cronos, his youngest brother, castrated him with a scythe provided by Gaia, which led to the 'Golden Age', a time of peace and harmony. These four brothers then represented the four pillars separating Earth from Heaven, with Iapetus representing the pillar of the West. Following the fall of Cronos, overthrown by his youngest son Zeus, commenced a battle known as the Titanomachy between the Titans and the younger Olympian gods. Zeus, being victorious, is said to have thrown the Titans who opposed him, including Iapetus, to Tartarus, whilst his son, Atlas, became the sole bearer of the weight of the sky.

Iapetus is often known as 'the Piercer', likely due to his prowess using a spear. He was known by the ancient Greeks as the god of mortality, and was seen as the father of mankind due his paternity of Epimetheus, who married Pandora, the first human woman, created by the Olympian god Hephaestus. There have also been suggestions that he is linked to Japheth, the third son of Noah, perhaps due to the similarity in his name, who is seen as the father of mankind in biblical traditions.

He is best known in modern reception as an anti-hero in the Percy Jackson series, who fights Percy but falls into the River Lethe where his memory is wiped and he is re-christened as 'Bob'. He later helps Percy and his girlfriend Annabeth through Tartarus, helped by his knowledge of the paths from his imprisonment by Zeus.

Saturn's third largest moon is also named in Iapetus' honour.

Rachel Stott

121

Coeus (Co)

❧ ━━━ ••• ━━━ ❧

Κοῖος | Coy-us / Kway-uss / Co-ay-uss

PERHAPS ONE OF THE lesser known figures of Greek mythology, Coeus was nevertheless respected by the ancient Greeks as a Titan. Coeus is often linked with intelligence and wisdom, being the smartest of Ouranos and Gaia's children.

Coeus was born when the Earth and Sky came together. As a Titan, Coeus' siblings included the father of the lightning God, Cronus, as well as Hyperion, Oceanus, and his lover Phoebe. With Phoebe, Coeus fathered Leto, who would later bring Artemis and Apollo into the world. In fact, Coeus is said to have the gift of prophecy; a gift he passed down to Apollo who would become the Oracle of Delphi.

Coeus' legacy lives on as one of the Titans who dethroned their father, Ouranos. He and three of his brothers held Ouranos down in the four corners of the world. Whilst restrained in this way, Ouranos was castrated by Cronus and thus was unable to couple with Gaia again.

Coeus' Roman counterpart is known as Polus. The story of Ouranos' downfall has Coeus positioned in the north and so 'Polus' alludes to the idea of Coeus representing the North Pole: the point in which the rest of the world spins while it remains steadfast. Quite appropriate for such an obscure figure to represent the illusive tundra of the Arctic.

The Greek island of Kos is attributed to Coeus, who is said to have been its first resident and where his daughter Leto was born.

Kenna Gibson

122

Oceanus (Oc)

❧〜•▬▬▬•••▬▬▬•〜❧

Ὠκεανός | Oh-she-ah-nuhs / O-key-ah-nuhs

To the ancient Greeks, Oceanus was the personification of the great freshwater river which encircled a disc-like earth. From Oceanus, all other fresh-water rivers, streams, and clouds drew their water – most through subterranean aquifers[1] but some, like the Underworld River Styx, directly from Oceanus's stream.

Oceanus was depicted in classical Greek iconography as an old man with a long beard, bull horns, and a serpentine tail in place of legs. In the Hellenistic era, Oceanus was reimagined as the god of the sea[2] and his horns replaced with crab claws. His body was otherwise imagined as a gigantic river which marked the end of civilisation. The ancient Greeks were in awe of anyone or anything brave enough to live close to Oceanus, as they saw him as unwieldy and impossibly vast.

Born of Gaia and Ouranus, Oceanus was the oldest of the Titans. Like Switzerland, Oceanus was all about neutrality, and abstained from both the castration of his father by his brothers, and the War between the Titans and the Olympian gods. Instead, Oceanus and his sister-wife Tethys spent their time producing 3000 sons (Potamoi)[3] and as many daughters (Oceanids)[4]. As the great river, the gods of the Sun, Moon, and Stars all had palaces within Oceanus, and he controlled when they rose and set within his waters.

Though not the most popular classical Greek figure of the modern day, Oceanus still plays a role in the broader legacy of Greek mythology across such fields as language, science, and popular culture.

References to Oceanus abound in brand names hoping to borrow some of the infinite mystery of the marine depths, and he also makes limited appearances in video games and fictional literature. The Titan's greatest contribution by far is the word by which we call a very large body of water, the ocean.

Madelaine Sacco

OCEANVS.

1.

123

Theia (Ta)

Θεία | Thay-ah / Thee-ah / Tay-ah

IN ANTIQUITY, THEIA WAS associated with sight and the light of the sky. She was also responsible for the brilliance of precious metals such as gold. Her name seems to be related to the ancient Greek words for sight and feminine divinity. One of the Titans, Theia was the eldest daughter of the primordial gods of the sky and earth, Ouranus and Gaia. Her consort was her brother Hyperion, himself associated with the sky and sun, and together they had three children; Helios the sun, Selene the moon, and Eos the dawn.

Called a goddess of many names by the 6th century BCE poet Pindar, Theia is referred to in the *Homeric Hymns* as Euryphaessa, wide-shining. In the much later *Fabulae* of Hyginus, she is called Aethra, the bright or blue sky. Her surviving mythological tradition is mostly concerned with her genealogical role as daughter and mother. One later account, however, refers to the mother of Selene as Basileia, an empress or queen. This telling relates that she was the most kind and responsible of the descendants of Ouranus and Gaia and thereby took on a motherly role in raising her male siblings, who later became jealous and caused the mortal death of her children Selene and Helios; an act that guaranteed that her two children would live on as the heavenly bodies of the moon and the sun.

Though mostly unknown to modern audiences, the hypothetical planet theorised to have collided with the earth billions of years ago bears the name of Theia. The collision is believed to have resulted in the formation of the moon, an appropriate reference to the mythological progenitor of the earth's natural satellite.

Robert Caudill

124

Themis (Te)

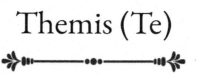

Θέμις | Thee-mis / Thehm-iss

T HEMIS IS THE TITAN goddess of justice, personification of law and order, and prophetic goddess associated with even the most ancient oracles. As one of the 12 Titans born to Ouranos and Gaia, she aided her siblings in the conquering of Ouranos, only to turn and side with the Olympians during the later Titanomachy. By joining the new gods and goddesses in the war against the other Titans, Themis secured her safety and was eventually married to Zeus, king of the gods himself; she is most notably the mother of the Moirae, more commonly known as the Fates, the Horae, and, in some sources, the mother of Prometheus. After her separation from Zeus, she remained on Mount Olympus serving as a counsellor to the king of the gods and presiding over the Olympian assemblies. She was consulted often to maintain the divine order on Mount Olympus thanks to her ability to see the truth.

To the ancient Greeks, Themis was a hugely important figure. She balanced the scales of justice, set the rules for mankind to live by, oversaw assemblies, and was closely connected to the oracles; especially the Oracle at Delphi, which she took care of between Gaia and Apollo, eventually going on to gift Apollo with prophecy. Themis even had temples dedicated to her throughout the ancient Greek world, with some dedicated to not only her, but the goddess Nemesis as well.

Themis still comes down to us today in more ways than one, but she is most commonly seen as a robed figure holding the scales of justice in paintings, on pottery, and more. She is more commonly known as "Lady Justice". Remains of one of her temples can still be found today in Athens, below the Parthenon. In mythology, she plays small parts in versions of Prometheus' story, Thetis' story, and even Deucalion and Pyrra.

Emily Bausher

THEMIS.

125

Mnemosyne (Mn)

〰〰〰

Μνημοσύνη | Neh-moh-sun-ee / Nee-moh-sun-ee

M NEMOSYNE, WHOSE NAME MEANS memory, was born of Gaia the Earth and Ouranos the Sky. She and her siblings, who include Cronus and Rhea among others, were known as the Titans.

Mnemosyne and Zeus are the parents of the Muses, the goddesses of inspiration. Some sources claim that Mnemosyne herself is one of the Muses, or part of an earlier set of Muses from before the written word.

As with her daughters, Mnemosyne is associated with inspiration and music. As the goddess of memory, it is likely that this association comes from the use of singing as a memory aid. Mnemosyne is also credited with the invention of language, naming, and even reason itself. In poetry, Mnemosyne is often evoked alongside her daughters to the aid of the poet, and generally praised for her wisdom. In philosophy, she appears to aid in argument and logic.

Mnemosyne was worshipped most often alongside her daughters at temples dedicated to the Muses, but also appears in conjunction with Apollo's oracles, who might "drink the water of Mnemosyne"[1] in order to recall visions, and with Asclepius, god of healing, so that the doctors might remember all they have learned.

Even now, we remember her name in our technology. There is a memorization tool called Mnemosyne, and her name appears in multiple video games as some type of technology or drug to store or gain access to information.

Julie Levy

Gioue si parte dal suo eterno tempio Et fatto u uil pastore aῆro. e ſſēp io
Per una Ninfa ch lo strugge e ſſace Ch ogni coſa ad Amor ſoggetta gi ace

.I. Bonaſone ſ̃ Inuentor

126

Phoebe (Ph)

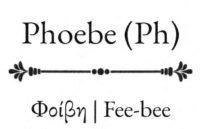

Φοίβη | Fee-bee

Pʜᴏᴇʙᴇ, ᴛʜᴇ Tɪᴛᴀɴ ɢᴏᴅᴅᴇss of intellect and prophecy, is the all-mighty Grandmother in Greek mythology. She stands among the first-generation Titanesses, meaning she was one of the twelve children of Ouranus and Gaia. The Titans – rulers of Earth before the Olympian gods – mainly resided on Mount Othrys until their banishment to the dark abyss of Tartarus. Unlike many of her fellow Titans, Phoebe remained unscathed after the Titanomachy, as she stayed neutral (mainly due to females not being allowed to fight). Her father and most of her brothers, however, were relegated to Tartarus.

She gave birth to two children with her brother-husband Coeus: Asteria and Leto. Asteria, in turn, became the mother of Hecate, while Leto brought Olympian gods, Artemis and Apollo into the world.

Brightness shone through Phoebe as not only was she the Titan goddess of intellect, but her name also derives from φοῖβος (phoîbos), which means "bright" or "shining". Apollo also adopted her name to become Apollo Phoebus which translates to the "Shining Apollo". He took this name in homage to his grandmother. In later mythology Phoebe was associated with the moon, as was her granddaughter, Artemis.

Phoebe's most enduring legacy, (besides her namesake writing the song *Smelly Cat* in the '90s sitcom *Friends*), lies in her ownership of the Oracle of Delphi. She was not only one of the holders of the Oracle, but she gifted her grandson, Apollo, the power of the Oracle for his birthday. The world-renowned temple is such an important part of Greek history and is still called the Temple of Apollo to this day.

Hesiod's *Theogony* bestows Phoebe's only epithet in which she is described as "gold-crowned".

Ella Quinn

127

Rhea (Rh)

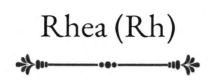

Ῥέα | Ree-ah / Ray-ah

CLOSELY ASSOCIATED WITH HER mother Gaia (Earth), Rhea was herself a mother goddess with ties to fertility. Her father was Ouranos (Sky) and her siblings were the Titans, Hecatoncheires, and the Cyclopes.

Rhea was consort to her brother Cronus, who castrated and usurped their father to become supreme ruler of the gods. From him she bore the first of the Olympians: Hestia, Demeter, Hera, Hades, Poseidon, and Zeus.

For fear of being overthrown like his father – as foretold in a prophecy – Cronus plotted to keep his seat as king of the gods. When Rhea gave birth to each of their children, he proceeded to eat them one by one. Their youngest child, Zeus, narrowly escaped being eaten, as Rhea gave birth to him in secret and hid the baby in a cave protected by Curetes[1]. The Curetes are said to have danced wildly about, clashing their shields to hide the cries of the infant. In place of baby Zeus, Rhea swaddled a stone for Cronus to swallow, who gulped it down just as he had his other children, oblivious to Rhea's trick.

Rhea kept Zeus hidden until he reached adulthood, when she plotted with him to retrieve the rest of her children from Cronus. After Zeus grew up, he forced his father to regurgitate his siblings and thus began a war between the newly freed Olympians, led by Zeus, and the Titans, led by Cronus. The Olympians, of course, came out victorious and imprisoned the Titans in Tartarus.

According to the Hellenistic poet Lycophron, Rhea was a skilled wrestler!

Echo Smith

128

Tethys (Ty)

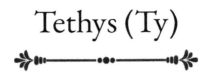

Τηθύς | Teth-iss / Teth-ees

NOT MUCH IS KNOWN about the first generation of the ancient Greek gods, outside of Cronus and Rhea, who were called the Titans. Tethys was part of that first generation. There is no evidence of a wider worship of her in ancient Greece. Tethys was Ouranus and Gaia's youngest girl and was the one before the last child, a boy: Cronus.

Zeus and the younger generation of gods are so popular that they overshadowed Tethys and the other Titans of the older generation, meaning Tethys has no active role in ancient Greek mythology. Tethys is primarily known as the consort of Oceanus, who is the personification of the ocean, and who in ancient times was thought to be a large river that circled the entire world.

She is the mother of many minor river gods, including the river god Nilus, the god of the River Nile in Egypt, a notable example of how Greek mythology and Egyptian mythology once intersected.

One of the few stories about her is in the *Iliad,* where Hera states that while Zeus was planning to dispose of their father Cronus, Rhea (their mother) sent a young Hera to the home of Tethys and Oceanus, who had nursed her and taken great care of her.

She is also briefly mentioned in the works of Ovid who states that she turned Aesacus into a diving bird, and in the works of Claudian who conveys that she nursed her nephew and niece Selene and Helios.

One of the moons on the planet Saturn (the Roman name for Cronus) is named after her. She is Saturn's fifth largest moon!

Princess O'Nika Auguste

Illustrations
In Order of Appearance

Cthonic Characters

1. Hendrick Goltzius. *Pluto*. 1594

2. Ludwig Mack. *Judges*. 1829

3. Nicolaes Braeu After Karel van Mander. *De godin Proserpina*. 1598

4. Cornelis Bloemaert. *Sisyphus*. 1655

5. Antonio Tempesta. *Hercules and Cerberus*. 1608

6. Stéphane Mallarmé. *Hecate*. 1880

7. Gustave Doré. *Canto III: Arrival of Charon*. 1857

8. Giulio Sanuto. *Tantalus*. ca. 1565

9. Cornelis Cornelisz. van Haarlem. *Ixion. De vier vallers*. 1588

10. Unknown. *Thanatos*. 1884

Women

1. Bernard Picart (workshop of). *Pandora's Box*. 1733

2. Francis Legatt Chantrey. *Penelope, sitting with Odysseus's armor*. ca. 1872

3. Jean Claude Danzel After François Boucher. *Neptune and Amymone*. 18th Century

4. Friedrich Preller the Elder. *Calypsos Abschied von Odysseus*. 1864

5. John Flaxman Jr. *Nausicaa ayant rencontré Ulysse sur le bord du fleuve*. 1810

6. Angelica Kauffmann. *Ariadne*. 1778

7. B. Luti. *Atalanta and Hippomanes*. 1791

Heroes

1. Johannes Hevelius. *Orion*. 1690

2. Jean-Baptiste Poncet. *Orphée*. ca. 1864

3. T. van Thulden After P.P. Rubens. *Bellerophon slaying the Chimera*. ca. 1640

4. Wilhelm Janson, Antonio Tempesta. *Jason Putting the Dragon to Sleep*. 1606

5. Antonio Tempesta. *Hercules and Cerberus*. 1608

6. Antonio Tempesta. *Perseus Killing Medusa*. 1606

Groups

1. Jacob Matham After Hendrick Goltzius. *The Three Fates*. 1587

2. G.B. Wicar after Giulio Romano. *Apollon et Les Muses*. 18th century

3. Antonio Tempesta. *Juno with the Furies*. 1606

Cyclopes

1. Mary Stansbury Ruiz Bequest. *Forge of the Cyclopes*. 1572

2. P. Sellier. *Tête de Médusa de la coupe Farnèse*. 1872

3. Antonio Tempesta. *Circe Changing Ulysses' Men into Swine*. 1606

4. Abraham van Diepenbeeck. *Atlas supporting the heavens*. ca. 1655

5. Cornelis Cort After Frans Floris the Elder. *Hercules Slaying the Hydra*. 1563

6. Hendrik Hondius I. *A Chimerical Animal Chasing Other Animals*. 1610

7. Antonio Tempesta. *Theseus and the Minotaur*. 1606

8. Hendrik Goltzius. *Apollo Killing the Python*. 17th Century

9. Gustave Doré. *Canto XIII: Harpies in the Forest of Suicides*. 1861

10. Antonio Tempesta. *Sirens of Perseophone turned into birds*. 1606

Transformations

1. Isidore Stanislas Helman After Charles Monnet. *Circé et Scylla*. 1771

2. Alessandro Allori. *Scylla and Charybdis*. 1575

3. Frans van der Neve. *Narcissus and Echo*. 17th Century

4. F. Kirchbach. *The Rape of Ganymede*. 1892

5. Crispijn van de Passe. *Jupiter and the Cow*. ca. 1604

6. Frans Floris. *Daphne*. 1564

7. Crispijn van de Passe. *Jupiter and Mercury visit Philemon and Baucis*. ca. 1604

8. Hendrick Goltzius (workshop of). *Deucalion and Pyrrha*. 1589

9. Hendrick Goltzius. *Diana discovers Callisto's Pregnancy*. 1599

10. Frans Floris (possibly). *Arachne*. 1574

11. Augustin de Saint-Aubin After François Boucher. *Diane au bain*. 1767

12. Antonio Tempesta. *Thisbe Killing Herself*. 1606

13. Francesco Bartolozzi After Giovanni Battista Cipriani. *Bas relief of Hermaphroditus*. 1787

14. Evedawn99. *Leucippus of Crete*. 2023

15. Johann Ulrich Krauß. *Tiresias Striking the Snakes*. ca. 1690

16. Antonio Tempesta. *Iphis*. 1606

17. Antonio Tempesta. *The Death of Niobe's Children*. 1606

18. Joachim von Sandrart the Elder. *Pygmalion*. 1662

Dramatis Personae

1. Claude Ferdinand Gaillard After Ingres. *Oedipus and the Sphinx*. 1690

2. Noël Le Mire After Charles Dominique Joseph Eisen. *Médée poignarde ses enfants*. 1768

3. Jean-Baptiste Blaise Simonet After Jean-Michel Moreau. *Oreste*. 1784

4. Giuseppe Diotti. *Testa di Creonte*. 19th Century

5. Aubrey Beardsley. *Lysistrata*. 1896

6. Sebastiano de Valentinis. *Prometheus*. ca. 1558

7. Jan Swart from Groningen. *Cassandra mourns the destruction of Troy*. 1550 - 1555

8. Emil Teschendorff. *Antigone and Ismene*. 1892

9. Giulio Romano. *Agamemnon killing Odios*. ca. 1545

10. Frédéric Lix. *Agamemnon assassiné par Clytemnestre*. 1862

11. Unknown. *Astianax Thrownin Front of Andromache*. 19th Century

12. Giulio Bonasone. *Bacchus*. 16th Century

13. Wilhelm von Kaulbach. *Iphigenia and Her Brother Orestes*. 1900

14. Unknown. *Xerxes crossing the Hellespont*. ca. 1882

Chaos

1. Hendrik Goltzius. *The Untangling of Chaos*. 1589

2. Karl Friedrich Schinkel. *Uranus*. 1845

3. Antonio Tempesta. *Creation of the World*. 1606

4. William-Adolphe Bouguereau. *Day*. 1884

5. James Basire. *The Orphic Egg*. 1774

6. Unknown. *Aion Mosaic*. 200-250

7. Abraham Ortelius. *Map of Crete*. 1584

8. Anselm Feuerbach. *Gaia*. 1875

9. Unknown. *Pontus*.

10. Carl Gustav Amling After Peter Candid. *Night*. 17th Century

11. Hendrick Goltzius. *Eros*. 16th Century

12. François-Guillaume Ménageot. *The Study Who Wants to Stop Time*. 18th Century

13. Unknown. *Aphrodite with Himeros*. 420-410 BC

The Trojan War

1. Unknown. *Roman Mosaic of Thalassa*. 5th Century

2. Paris Gille. *Judgement of Paris*. 1694

3. Antonio Tempesta. *Hecuba and the Trojan Women Murdering Polymestor*. 1606

4. Giulio Romano. *Menelaus Holding the Body of Patroclus*. 16th Century

5. Lucas Vorsterman II. *Achilles and Priam*. ca. 1644–66

6. Helen Maitland Armstrong. *Helen*. ca. 1903

7. Hy. Fuseli R.A.. *Odysseus Slaying the Suitors*. 1806

8. Nicolaes de Bruyn. *Portrait of Hector of Troy*. 1594

9. François Boucher. *Venus and Aeneas*. 18th Century

10. Wilhelm Bauer. *Suicide of Ajax*. 17th Century

11. Giulio Romano. *Battle around the Body of Patroclus*. ca. 1543

12. Mezzotint after G. Hamilton. *Achilles Dragging the Body of Hector*. 1794

Olympians

1. Hendrik Goltzius. *Jupiter*. 1592

2. Pieter Mortier. *Poseidon*. 1703

3. Hendrick Goltzius. *Minerva asks Envy to incite jealousy*. 1590

4. D. Sornique after J. Boulogne. *Artemis and Actaeon*. 18th Century

5. Willem Isaacsz Swanenburg. *Aphrodite*. 1595 - 1612

6. Master I.B. *Mercury*. 1528

7. Giulio Bonasone. *Juno watching Jupiter and Io*. 1531 - 1560

8. Salvator Rosa. *Ceres and Phytalus*. 1662

9. Jacob Matham after Hendrik Goltzius. *Apollo*. ca. 1597

10. Jacques Jonghelinck. *Ares*. 1585

11. Raffaello Guidi. *Hephaestus*. 1613

12. Jan van Vianen. *Vesta*. 1697

Titans

1. Johann Ladenspelder. *Saturn*. 16th Century

2. Cornelis van Haarlem. *The Fall of the Titans*. 1588–1590

3. Unknown. *Flammarion Engraving*. 1888

4. Georges Reverdy. *Japeth*. 1553

5. Gustave Doré. *Canto XXXI: The titans and giants*. 1857

6. Philip Galle. *Oceanus.* 1586

7. Unknown. *Theia from Pergamon Altar.* 200-150 BC

8. Unknown. *Themis.* 1878

9. Giulio Bonasone. *Jupiter and Mnemosyne.* 1531–1576

10. John Flaxman Jr. *To Phoebus at His Birth.* Late 18th Century

11. Unknown. *Kronos and his wife Rhea.* 100-200 AD

12. Hendrick Goltzius. *Tethys. Goddess of the Waters.* ca. 1590

Endnotes

Hades (H)

1. Literally, 'gods of the earth'.

2. Literally "a descent", a *catabasis* is a journey to the underworld, often undertaken by a hero or semi-divine figure (such as Heracles, Orpheus etc).

3. Connecting him with *ploutos,* "wealth".

4. The Mysteries represented the story of Persephone's abduction from her mother Demeter by the king of the underworld Hades, in a cycle with three phases.

5. A "horn of plenty": a large goat's horn that is filled with agricultural bounty such as flowers, fruit and wheat.

Sisyphus (Sp)

1. Also known as Corinth.

2. The Ancient Greek concept of hospitality – Xenia refers to the ancient Hellenic practice of guest right, a sacred binding of host to guest, of receiving a stranger as if they are a disguised deity testing one's piety. Characterised by generosity and reciprocity, it has its modern equivalent in the Isles today.

3. The deepest place in Hades where the worst of the gods and men are punished for eternity.

4. Thinking oneself as equal to the gods themselves, or trying to best them in some way. A fatal theme which shows up in many Greek myths.

Hecate (Hc)

1. The Hellenistic Period is considered to be between 323BCE - 30BCE, while the Roman Period falls between the founding of Rome in 625BCE and its fall in 476CE.

Charon (Cr)

1. An ancient Greek coin.

2. A journey into the underworld.

Tantalus (Tn)

1. A region in modern day Turkey.

2. The home of the gods.

3. The food and drink of the gods.

Ixion (Ix)

1. A people living in Thessaly.

2. War between the centaurs and the Lapiths.

Pandora (Pn)

1. All quotes taken from Hesiod *Works & Days*.

Penelope (Pp)

1. According to the Greek geographer Pausanias.

2. An adjective repeatedly used to express a particular trait.

Amymone (Ay)

1. Father of Palamedes.

2. Hercules killed the Hydra in this river.

Atalanta (Al)

1. Exposure was a practice of infanticide that involved abandoning children to the natural elements to die of starvation, hypothermia, thirst, or animal attack. Not all children exposed died and were picked up by other families who could not bear their own children.

2. They made the mistake of making love inside the goddess's temple.

Orion (On)

1. Homer's *Iliad* describes Orion as a constellation. In the *Odyssey*, Orion is the pinnacle of human excellence in hunting. In the *Works and Days* of Hesiod the constellation's rising and setting with the sun is used to reckon the year.

2. Latin for 'greater dog' and 'lesser dog'.

3. Seven sister-nymphs and companions of Artemis.

Jason (J)

1. A land on the eastern shore of the Black Sea.

Heracles (Hk)

1. Often referred to today by his Roman name, Hercules.

2. Half-mortal, half-divine.

3. 'Invocation' is the act of using someone's name as a part of a charm, prayer, or other religious ritual to call upon that being's particular powers or qualities.

Perseus (Pe)

1. Creatures with snakes for hair who turned onlookers into stone.

2. Nymphs of the evening.

3. Sisters who shared one eye and one tooth.

4. Daughter of the King of Aethiopia.

Fates (F)

1. Western Turkey.

Muses (Mu)

1. The genealogy, names, and number of the Muses is not the same in all sources.

2. The transmission of knowledge from one generation to another without the aid of writing.

3. 'O, for a muse of fire that would ascend...' (Shakespeare, c.1599)

Cyclopes (Cs)

1. From fossil remains, we now know that dwarf elephants, *Palaeoloxodon* sp. lived on Malta, Sicily, Crete, Delos, Naxos, Paros, Kythnos, Milos, Serifos, Astypalaia, Kasos, Rhodes, Tilos, and Cyprus. Dwarf mammoths, *Mammutus creticus* shared the island of Crete with the aforementioned tiny elephants. Yet another species of dwarf mammoth, *Mammuthus lamarmorai*, lived on Sardinia.

Medusa (Ms)

1. King of Seriphos.

2. The "ægis" was the magical breastplate or shield of Zeus, which is given or lent to Athena.

Circe (Cc)

1. The Laistrygonians were a group of man-eating giants encountered by Odysseus on his journey.

Atlas (Aa)

1. The ten-year war between the newer Greek gods and the Titans.

Hydra (Lh)

1. Located south of Argos, on the Peloponnese.

2. Its siblings being Orthus, Cerberus, Chimaera, Sphinx, and the Nemean Lion.

3. Heracles would, himself, be killed when he unwittingly put on a tunic covered in the Hydra's blood.

4. Sealing a bodily wound with fire.

Minotaur (M)

1. Myths of legendary founders. Theseus wasn't supposed to have founded Athens himself, but he was thought to have played a key part in its unification.

2. Theseus was worshipped, but only in Athens.

Python (Py)

1. Such as a shrine.

2. The Greeks appeared to be uncertain about the gender of the Python, with the Homeric hymn referring to it as female, but other sources referring to it as male.

3. Priestesses of the god Apollo, often depicted in Greek art, sat on a large tripod.

Harpies (Hr)

1. A central public square in ancient Greek cities.

2. Also known as The Furies, the three goddesses of revenge and retribution.

3. An offensive term meaning shrill, foul and angry woman.

Sirens (Sn)

1. Bird-like.

Scylla (Sy)

1. Nymphs who live in or near water.

Echo and Narcissus (En)

1. Another name for a Mountain/Tree nymph. Literally means "those who live in the trees".

2. Modern Greek Voiotía, in central Greece. Home to the city Thebes.

3. Tiresias is seen in multiple Greek tragedies such as *Oedipus Rex, Antigone, The Bacchae,* and *The Odyssey.* His words were often ignored, but foreshadowed what would be the character's downfall.

4. Another version of the tale says Echo just hid in shame from his rejection, not called upon the god. Narcissus had rejected many nymphs and men including Ameinias, who prayed to Nemesis.

5. Styx was the goddess and river of the Underworld.

6. Ovid's *Metamorphoses* 3.500-510.

Ganymede (Gy)

1. A Phrygian cap was a soft conical cap with the top pulled forward and was associated with people from Eastern Europe, where Troy was located. A rooster represented an amorous gift from a male admirer, and the hoop and lyre were associated with youthful leisure.

Callisto (Cl)

1. A minor female deity, normally associated with nature.

2. The transformation of a heroic figure into a celestial body.

Arachne (S)

1. Latin poem written by the poet Ovid which narrates the history of the world.

2. Lydia was a kingdom located in western Asia Minor.

3. These episodes are very common in ancient mythology, with Zeus being one of the most popular perpetrators of such behaviour.

4. In Portuguese, a spider is called "Aranha"; in Spanish, "Araña", and in French "Araignée" and so on.

Hermaphroditus (Hd)

1. The god Attis also has male and female characteristics, but has the opposite!

Leucippus (Le)

1. Not the same Galatea who was turned from a statue into a human by the goddess Aphrodite.

Tiresias (Tr)

1. *The Theban Plays* by Sophocles, *The Bacchae* by Euripides, *Metamorphoses* by Ovid.

2. From Ovid's *Metamorphoses*, book 3, lines 316-338. Jupiter stated that women derive more pleasure in sex than men – Juno disagreed.

Medea (Md)

1. An Underworld goddess of magic, witchcraft and ghosts, often depicted with three faces.

2. King Pelias was Jason's uncle who ruled Iolcus and set Jason the task of securing the Golden Fleece.

Creon (Cn)

1. A powerful, treacherous mythical creature with the head of a human, the body of a lion, and the wings of an eagle.

2. 'What goes on four legs in the morning, two in the afternoon, and three in the evening?' The answer is 'human beings': they crawl as babies, walk as adults, and need a walking stick when old.

3. The most important oracle of ancient Greece from which Apollo gave prophecies and answers.

4. Ancient Greeks believed that denying burial prevented a person's soul from entering the afterlife, condemning them to an eternity of pain.

Agamemnon (Am)

1. Someone with the ability to see the future and converse with the Gods.

Clytemnestra (Ct)

1. Aeschylus' *Oresteia* is significant, as the only intact trilogy of tragedies.

Andromache (Ad)

1. Men hold the power and women have none.

Dionysus (Dy)

1. From the legend of the Tyrrhenian pirates in the Homeric *Hymn To Dionysus 7*, and Euripedes' play, *The Bacchae*.

2. A staff or spear tipped with an ornament like a pine cone.

3. A form of tunic that fastens at the shoulder.

4. The Mystery Cult of Dionysus involved many rituals in which the worshippers felt possessed by Dionysus.

Iphigenia (Ih)

1. Aulis was a port town in central Greece.

Ouranos (Ou)

1. Three terrifying giants of enormous might, each with fifty heads and 100 arms.

Hemera (Hm)

1. Personification gives a thing, an idea, or an abstract concept the character and form of a person, with human attributes and appearance.

Ophion (Op)

1. Origin story.

2. Resembling a snake.

Aion (Ao)

1. Secretive cults or religious groups who practised private initiations and rituals.

Gaia (G)

1. The implication is that he pushed them back inside their mother.

Pontus (Pu)

1. Ancient Greek word meaning "first born" in this case, first born gods.

2. Mythical sorcerers and artisans who inhabited the Island of Rhodes in the Mediterranean Sea.

Himeros (Ho)

1. A group of winged gods associated with love and sexual intercourse.

Hecuba (Hu)

1. From κυνὸς and σῆμα which mean "of the dog" and "mark" respectively. Cynossema would be the site of a naval battle between the Athenians and the Spartans during the Second Peloponnesian War.

Menelaus (Ml)

1. The Greeks' name during the events of the Trojan war, it is the oldest name for the Greeks. Other names are the Aeolians, Dorians and Ionians.

Odysseus (Oy)

1. A Greek island, which is likely the same as modern-day Ithaca off the north-east coast of Cephalonia.

2. Odysseus is also said to have had another son by the sorceress Circe, Telegonus.

3. A wooden statue of Athena that was the talisman of Troy and was said to be the key to victory over the city.

Ajax (Aj)

1. Another name for Troy and where the Iliad gets its title.

2. [Moment of] excellence where a single warrior dominates the battle, generally in an offensive push against the enemy or in some cases the gods themselves.

Zeus (Z)

1. To show or treat an animal, god, or object as if it is human in appearance, character, or behaviour.

2. Children.

3. The ancient Greeks believe the gods spoke directly through Oracles, but in this case, it just means 'prophecy'.

Poseidon (Po)

1. But only if you're 18 or over!

Athena (A)

1. Protector of the city.

2. Athena the Virgin.

3. 'Virgin-birth' seen in some animal species.

Aphrodite (Ah)

1. A Mesopotamian goddess.

2. A Canaanite goddess.

3. One of the mythical founders of Rome.

Hermes (He)

1. See *Flash Comics #1* (1940).

Apollo (Ap)

1. The lyre is a musical instrument gifted to Apollo by his brother Hermes, which is said to have been formed of a hollowed-out tortoiseshell and strings.

2. Ravens were commonly associated with prophecy in ancient Greece, and in mythology, the raven was a messenger of Apollo.

3. In the *Homeric Hymn to Apollo*, we are told that Apollo initially delivered oracles from a laurel tree at Delphi (3.396). In contrast, it could be argued that laurel represented victory, as Callimachus tells us that after Apollo's defeat of Python, he purified himself in the river Peneus, cut a nearby laurel, and made a wreath that he wore upon return to Delphi. Another possibility is that the laurel was associated with the myth of Apollo and Daphne. While there are various possibilities, what can be said for sure is that Apollo was associated with laurel.

4. Representative of Apollo's abilities as an archer.

Hephaestus (Hp)

1. A sea-nymph.

2. The Maenads were women who devoted themselves to Dionysos and often entered into a frenzied state. The Satyrs were half-man and half-human hybrids, often combining human bodies with donkey, pig or goat features.

3. Robots.

Hestia (Hs)

1. Something presented or offered to a god/goddess.

2. An aromatic sub-tropical flowering plant also known as 'Vitex' or 'Monk's Pepper'.

Cronos (T)

1. This is a quote from the Roman poet Ovid's *Metamorphoses,* which has been repeatedmany times in later Latin literature, especially the Medieval period. The literal translation is "Time,glutinous of all things" but it is more commonly translated as "time, consumer all things".

2. The Kronia was later known as Saturnalia by the Romans which was replaced by Christmas whenRome converted to Christianity under the emperor Constantine in 313 AD.

Crius (Ci)

1. The first of five ages of man.

2. Aries is the Ram in the Zodiac.

3. Birth of Aphrodite.

Hyperion (Hy)

1. From the Greek words *hyper* and *ion* which mean 'the high one'.

2. Hyperion's and his brother Iapetos, Crios, and Coeus were each assigned corners of the Earth (North, South, East and West) and represented pillars that separated the Earth and Heavens.

3. The personification of the Sun – also known as 'Hyperion' in ancient texts.

4. The personification of the Moon – called the 'bright-tressed'.

5. The personification of Dawn – often mentioned with the epithet 'rosy-fingered' by Homer.

Oceanus (Oc)

1. An underground layer of rock or sediment which holds water.

2. Pontus was the first personification of the sea. In the late classical era, Pontus was equated to Oceanus on account of Greek explorers discovering the sea was actually salty.

3. Minor gods of rivers and streams.

4. Minor goddesses of small streams, clouds, and rain.

Mnemosyne (Mn)

   1. A commonly used phrase in the Orphic mysteries.

Rhea (Rh)

   1. Young male armoured warriors or dancers of Crete, often associated with Rhea.

Printed in Great Britain
by Amazon

56146050R00163